The Way of the Sacred Pipe

The care and use of the Native American Sacred Pipe

By Jim Tree

"The Way of the Sacred Pipe" First edition copyright © 2004
James Medicine Tree

Published by
Blue Sky Publishing
PO Box 103
Hamilton, MT. 59840

Cover design by author, earth photo by NASA.

Photo credits:

The photographs on pages 51, 58,103, as well as the historical
photographs, are from the internet and are public domain.

The photographs on pages 37, 46, 47, 54, 64, are from the web site
of the "Keepers of the Sacred Tradition of Pipemakers."

The top photograph on page 88 Reggie Boyd

The rest of the photographs are the author's.

Editors: Valerie Barzetti, Shannon Barr, and Kathy Mensing

Library of Congress Catalog Number: 2006921910

ISBN: 0-9777820-0-X   13/ISBN: 978-0-9777820-0-0

Printed in the United States of America

Table of Contents

Dedication

This book was inspired by Kate, a 14-year-old girl I met in Pipestone, MN. I was attending the annual gathering of the *Keepers of the Sacred Tradition of Pipe Makers* and Kate, with her "wisdom beyond her years", gave me amazing hope for our future. As a few of us learned various Pipe ceremonies from Adam Fortunate Eagle, Kate amazed us with her comments and questions. Like so many kids today, she seemed to have a depth of understanding of the spiritual that far exceeded her life experience.

Ernest Thompson Seton, the renowned naturalist from the early 1900's, set the pace early in my life with his writings. When asked why he wrote, his statement was, "*I have known the torment of thirst; therefore, I dug a well so others may drink.*" Encouraged by his example, I decided to put into writing what I have learned in order to pass on to future generations the "uncommon assistance" that has been my fortunate experience. Kate's comments and questions clearly indicated to me these ancient ways are indeed the hope of this planet's future. I dedicate this book to humanity's future, the children like Kate.

Kate from Pipestone, 2003

In addition to Kate from Pipestone, I wish to also express my appreciation to the many others who have been instrumental in the path that has lead to the writing of this book.

First and foremost, to my children. They have been my greatest teachers. To my son David I dedicate the chapter *"The Power of the Pipe."* To my son Eric I offer the chapter *"What is the Native Mind?"* To my son Greg I give *"The Age of the Pipe."* And to my daughter Katherine I give the chapter *"Male and Female Pipes."* To my brothers George and Glenn and to my sister Anne, I offer *"Letting go of the Pipe."*

I wish to express my appreciation to both my parents for giving me a love for the natural world and for encouraging me to explore and always think for myself, using respectful skepticism when presented with "truth."

There are those who, throughout the years, have had a tremendous impact on my life and spiritual experience. I wish to acknowledge them for the patience and kind assistance offered to me as I have progressed on my journey.

To Adam Fortunate Eagle, who encouraged me to carve Pipes, I offer the chapter *"Gifts and Honors."* To Dr. Tamzon "Grace" Feeney, my true *Hunka* sister, I give the chapter *"Unity in Diversity."* To the late Lilly "Grandmother Windrider" Nevarez, I dedicate the chapter *"About Valerie."* To the late Larry War Eagle, my Cherokee spiritual advisor, I dedicate *"The Ineffective Pipe."*

Without my editors this book never would have become a presentable work. I offer to Shannon the chapter *"Tobacco and Prayer Ties"*, and to the late Valerie Barzetti I dedicate *"Is the Pipe for you?"*

I want to acknowledge Lora. It is she who created the long awaited bag for my personal Pipe. To her I offer the chapter *"Pipe Accessories."* And finally, I want to give *"What is the Pipe?"* to my best friend, Aimee, who healed a wound so deep no other could touch it. If not for her, I never would have had the courage to write this book.

6

Preface

Traditionally, understanding the way of the Sacred Pipe was acquired through one's upbringing, in a society where its use was a prominent part of daily life. The way of the Pipe was taught slowly, through continued participation in ceremonies where it was used. It took time and commitment to learn all that was needed in order to care for and use the Pipe properly. It was *and is* knowledge that should be passed on carefully and prayerfully.

Recently, the Sacred Pipe has become available world-wide to people who have had little or no real exposure to what it is or what it can do. People are buying Pipes in shops and over the Internet regularly. Some may have learned a little about the way of the Pipe by seeing it used at a ceremony or through a book, but seldom does this make them aware of what the Pipe really is.

I have researched the books available about the Pipe, some of which are very good. However, I have not found any that addresses the nature of the *living Pipe*. Some books tell how to perform a ceremony, or give some basics of the care of a Pipe, but I have found none that explains those things I feel are vital for anyone who wishes to use the Pipe. Because of the current situation, I feel it has become important that this information be made available in written form. It is my hope that, in doing so, it may stem the trend of misuse of this sacred and powerful gift we received from the Great Mystery so long ago.

It must be understood that using the Pipe is a *way of life*, not something you just do once in awhile. The misuse or even the lack of proper care of the Pipe can cause many severe and detrimental things to happen, just as the proper use and care can lead you to become the highest expression of the unique wonder you were created to be.

For those who question the photographing of the sacred or putting it into writing, there are many examples of guardians of these ways, who felt called to put them into printed form or allowed photographs to be taken.

Washakie   *Red Cloud*

While it unfortunately is true that we are in a time of unprecedented misuse of the sacred teachings of the Native American peoples worldwide, there are also those who felt it important to pass on the authentic teachings, before they are lost or distorted, through the written word.

These examples include such respected men as Nicolas Black Elk, Frank Fools Crow and Dr. Charles Eastman (Ohiyesa).

I realize there are many who will be against this book going to print. I have listened to concerns expressed by several people whom I respect. I understand also that these sacred ways have survived until today because they were protected over the centuries. They were kept hidden from the public, and strict rules concerning the procedures of ceremony were followed. You will see over and over in this book, my references about not being too constrained by the "rules." It is a very delicate balance to maintain age-old traditions, and also be open to the guidance of Spirit in the present situation. If it were not for my faith in the power of the Pipe to protect itself, I would not make this information available.

There are three reasons why I have decided to make this information available to the general public. The first reason is that which I have stated previously. Pipes are falling into the hands of people who do not have access to someone to show them these ways. I do not believe we can stop the Pipe's availability. It is something that is predestined, this is discussed in chapter one, *"The Age of the Pipe."*

Secondly, we are not living in the same times and situations that warranted secrecy before. We are in a very transitional time - a time when Pipes are turning up all around the world working toward a new way of existing for mankind. Thirdly, and most importantly, I am writing this book because I feel guided by the Great Mystery to do so. No one can say what another's directive from the Divine is, and I alone will stand responsible for the outcome of publishing this information. I have spent much time in prayer and meditation about this, and after all input was considered, I felt it was the will of both the Sacred Pipe and the Great Mystery to print this book. The understanding that an individual is able to hear from the Creator without the intervention of other people is at the very core of indigenous spirituality. It is more about trusting the Power of the Pipe to communicate than trusting the individual's ability to hear. If you truly know the Pipe is a powerful spiritual being, then you also know I stand accountable to it, not to any person.

The purpose of this book is to inform people interested in the proper use and care of a personal Sacred Pipe, but *not* that of a Ceremonial Pipe. The differences between a personal Pipe and a Ceremonial Pipe will be discussed, but the ways of the Ceremonial Pipe can *only* be passed on through actual experience and apprenticeship.

Some who read this book may complain that I am presenting "pan-Indian" religion, that is, a mix of several tribes' beliefs. I am a non- enrolled Cherokee, but I was introduced to the

Sacred Pipe through the *Anishinobie* (Chippewa), and have had further exposure through the Lakota and Apache, as well as other tribes.

Although I am Cherokee, I do not represent just Cherokee ways. I share things in this book that have helped me along my path of life. The sweat lodge and *Sundance* ceremonies are not Cherokee traditions; however they have been powerful influences in my life, used by the Great Mystery to heal and help me. I represent only my own personal path, the path of life that I have walked to this point.

Several years ago, I attended a large gathering of Native men high in the mountains of central Colorado. Before the gathering, Elders, representing 110 of the tribes still active in North America, had met and discussed the need for a simple guide for Native men, based on the common traditions of each tribe. What they came up with was the *Seven Philosophies for Native Men,* which were taught to us at the gathering, and have since been distributed in written form to thousands of others. Although there are many different teachings on how to be a traditional tribal man, the *Seven Philosophies* present only the commonalities among all tribes.

In a very small way, I am using the same approach with this book. I am presenting the common ways to use and care for the Sacred Pipe, focusing on the *commonalities* of the Pipe, found throughout the many traditions of the original people of this continent. Throughout the book, I draw upon those traditions of a specific tribe that most clearly describe what I am trying to explain.

An example of this would be the words used to describe the Sacred Pipe. In Cherokee, *Ganvnawa* is the word used for an assembled Pipe; however, in Lakota there is a word for both the bowl and the stem of the Pipe. As well, I use the Lakota terms when describing the spiritual elements of both the male and female parts of the Pipe. In using examples and words from different traditions, I am not advocating mixing of the spirituality of different tribes. Rather, I am relating to you the way of the Pipe from my personal experience.

An important point I would like to make is the ceremonial descriptions in this book do not reveal any *secrets*. You could try to duplicate the ceremonies, but they would not work for you. All ceremonies of power are revealed to an individual by his or her own particular spiritual helpers. What works for me, to say, split the rain clouds, may not work for you. For you to have the medicine to do this would require that the spirits show you how they want you to do it. Why? Because as you will see presented time and again in this writing, real spirituality is based on an ongoing relationship with the Divine, not on pre-described dogmatic incantations, so to speak.

We are now in the prophesied *Age of the Pipe* (see chapter one) and the Pipes are already spreading around the earth. Should we not do what we can to ensure they are cared for in the best way possible? In writing this book, I hope that I may honor those Elders mentioned previously as well as the Spirit of the Sacred Pipe itself.

Adam Fortunate Eagle passing on the Ways of the Sacred Pipe to Tim, a young Cherokee Pipe carver who lives in Austria. Pipes are truly being spread around the world

11

Chief Bob, Turtle, Larry War Eagle, Doc, Griz and the Author

The Sacred Pipe is central to most Native American spirituality, and my hope is this information will help bring the blessing it summons to all the children of our Mother Earth. In the words of my Chief, Bob Strong Bear, "If everyone in the world had a personal Pipe and used it in the proper way, we would truly have peace and harmony today." That is a pretty powerful statement, but once you understand the possibilities, you might just agree.

James Medicine Tree
January 2004

A special note: The One to whom we offer up the smoke of the Pipe (i.e. our requests or prayers) will be referred to as the **Great Mystery**. This One is known by many descriptions, all of which are designed to help us relate to it through our own limitations. Names such as God, Creator, Grandfather, Father, Mother, Spirit, etc. are all used, but I prefer the term "Great Mystery" as it best describes *for me* the amazing entity who has chosen to give us this means (the Pipe) of making our requests known to it.

12

Chapter 1
Pipe Basics

Owl in Tree, Woodlands style Pipe

The Age of the Pipe

There is an ancient prophecy that the time would come, after seven generations of subjugation by a white serpent that came from across the great eastern waters, when the children of the Earth, from all four directions, would come to the Elders of the Native Americans to learn the ways of harmony. This prophecy was to mark the time of the birth of a new world, the age/world of interdependence and lasting peace.

A more recent version of this prophecy was given in a vision to Crazy Horse, the great Lakota leader. He shared this vision to Sitting Bull during a Pipe ceremony, just four days before he was murdered.

"Upon suffering beyond suffering; the Red Nation shall rise again and it shall be a blessing for a sick world. A world filled with broken promises, selfishness and separations. A world longing for light again. I see a time of seven generations when all the colors of mankind will gather under the sacred Tree of Life and the whole Earth will become one circle again. In that day there will be those among the Lakota who will carry knowledge and understanding of unity among all living things, and the young white ones will come

13

to those of my people and ask for this wisdom. I salute the light within your eyes where the whole universe dwells. For when you are at that center within you and I am that place within me, we shall be as one." -- Crazy Horse

We have seen the beginning of the fulfillment of this prophesy over the last few decades here on Turtle Island (North America), with the increase of young people of all four colors of humankind finding peace and purpose through walking in our ways. Unfortunately, with this world-wide increase in interest in Native American ways and spirituality, there has been an equal increase in misinformation about our ways, sometimes intentional, sometimes not, and many times with unfortunate consequences.

Using a Sacred Pipe without knowing its power or purpose is like obtaining a weapon but not understanding what it is capable of, especially if misused. Trying to access the medicine of the Pipe without proper understanding can be as dangerous as playing with a loaded gun. Someone usually gets hurt, often a loved one. Once again, I emphasize the Pipe is much more than just a powerful instrument to access the attention of the Divine. It is intended to become the residence of a beneficial Spirit, who comes to us to teach, protect, provide and intercede for us. As beneficial as a well cared for Pipe can be, improper care or use of such a powerful sacred object can be disastrous.

Part of the prophecy mentioned previously tells of the *Age of the Pipe*. We are living at a time when old Pipes are resurfacing and new Pipes are being created to be awakened not only here in North America, but all around the world. These Pipes are integral to the ushering in of this way of interdependence of all races. It is through the Pipe that the Great Mystery has made available a way to restore harmony to all things. This is why they are being dispersed throughout the world, their positive energies and effects interlacing like a giant spider web covering the planet.

Recently it has been interpreted the promised "web" that will cover the globe is the Internet, but as we have seen, it is just another amazing tool created by humans. It has vast potential, but due to the inherent weakness of people, it fails to deliver the promised harmony. The Sacred Pipe was created by the Great Mystery, and is above human weakness, being a higher form of expression of the Great Mystery than we are. It has its place of function, just as we humans do. As each part of Creation rediscovers its proper function, this new world is possible.

I am sure there are other items of a similar and equal spiritual nature as the Pipe coming forth at this time, all to promote harmony according to their various spiritual ways. *Interdependence* is what we are learning from all the various traditions. Again, the way of the Pipe is not for everyone, but for those who are called into this sacred relationship, there is nothing more powerful in this dimension for accessing the Divine.

The Power of the Pipe

I want to tell you the history of a Ceremonial Pipe that came into my care a few years ago. The reason for this is to introduce you to just how powerful and effective the Sacred Pipe actually is. Lakota Holy Man, Frank Fools Crow, said that miracles do not make believers, but I hope after reading these accounts you will at least receive the idea that you are being introduced to something that can bring "uncommon assistance" into your life.

To start with, let me say something that has helped me tremendously in sorting out what things are of true spiritual value. Today there is so much out there claiming to be spiritual truth. It is confusing, to say the least. Here is my "formula" in sorting out the *real from the fake*, or in my terms, the *spiritual from the religious:*

"If it is real, it works; if it works, it is real."

15

In other words, if something has, say, healing power, it *will* heal, not because of my faith in it to heal, but because it has the actual power within itself to heal.

I have followed the spiritual path, commonly known as the "Red Road" (White Road to the Cherokee), most of my life. The Red Road is most easily described as *conducting your life in a way that puts you in harmony with all of creation.* This spiritual path is based on the understanding that we are all part of the great circle of life, and being "spiritual" means finding our place and proper function in this circle. All places in the circle are of equal importance, none is above the others.

All faiths, including the Red Road, can be a dogmatic activity devoid of actual true spiritual activity, i.e. spiritual activity that produces tangible/practical results, not just pie in the sky.) The Red Road is a nature-based faith. If you separate its ways and ceremonies from nature, all you have left is just another religion. Just as true spirituality can be found in *any* faith, dogma can be found in any religion as well. Unfortunately, it is a human tendency that the roots of dogma spring forth from all true divine inspiration.

Nature is not under the control of humans; therefore, there is a reality to the Red Road that is often absent in other spiritual paths. It is one thing to call on the Spirit of Owl to assist with a ceremony; it is quite another thing to have owls actually arrive when summoned to a ceremony.

A central part of the traditional ways of Native peoples is the use of the Sacred Pipe to assist us in our walk. It is understood this Pipe is not just an instrument for ceremony, but an actual living spirit entity that comes into our lives to teach, guide, protect and nurture us. Many pre-contact Native American nations had the tradition where most adults possessed a personal Pipe. As I will explain later, a personal Pipe is similar in power to the Ceremonial Pipe, but its work is that of assisting an individual, rather than being used in ceremonies to assist a nation.

So, if you find yourself on this spiritual journey, which would you chose to reach the destination, a map or a guide?

This book is just a map, the Pipe is a guide. A map, such as a written Manuscript or scripture, can be misinterpreted without the proper training to read it. Or if the map is not an original, it may have been re-drawn/translated over the centuries with the possibility of inaccuracies. A living guide such as the spirit/angel that dwells in the Pipe) knows the way to harmony and can lead you to the destination. I, personally, prefer the guide.

I will use terms relating to the Pipe such as, "I heard the Pipe" or "the Pipe said." You may wonder what I mean by this. Does the Pipe have an audible voice? Yes and no. The Pipe speaks to each of us a bit differently.

When the Pipe speaks to me, it is usually through one of two ways. The first is through a voice I hear in my mind. Often it is more of a complete thought, rather than sentences or a progression of thought. I have learned to identify the Pipe's "voice" from that of my own thoughts through trial and error. I will just say that when I "hear" the Pipe speak, it is always with definable results that match the communication given. I have actually heard an audible voice on occasion, but more often it is similar to a married couple who seem to be able to read each other's thoughts without actually saying anything.

The second way the Pipe speaks to me is through "coincidence." An example of this is when I sent a Pipe to Don, a good friend of mine. When he went to open the package containing the Pipe, he pulled a lighter out of his pocket while looking for a knife. He placed the lighter on the box and it "jumped" off, twice in a row! This was the Pipe's way of telling him it did not want to be lit by a butane lighter. I always pay close attention to things that happen around a Pipe or during a ceremony.

Once, when I did a naming ceremony for a little Cherokee girl, I planned to use my son's medicine staff as part of the ceremony. As I stuck the staff into the ground, the bottom of it broke off. I saw this as the Pipe's way of saying not to do what I normally would. Instead of planting the staff in the ground as usual, I handed the staff to the little Dira. What she did with it became part of the ceremony. She passed it over to another child who was attending the ceremony, and I saw "medicine" going into the boy from the staff. This would not have happened if I had not listened to the Pipe (circumstances), and instead performed the ceremony according to the "rules."

Now, let me describe the Pipe I will be telling you about in this section. It is made of Black Pipestone (steatite), and has lead inlay in the form of two thunderbirds on its bowl. It has been handed down for at least three generations, making it over 200 years old. Its medicine or mission is to connect with the Thunder Beings (those Spirits that control the weather) and to perform healings. It has, in recent history, broken a seven-year drought, as well as many other amazing things which I will relate to you. I want to point out right here that power is in the Pipe, not the one who takes care of it.

I also need to preface this history with a brief account of my own story before this Pipe came into my care. This is to help you understand why it came to me, and not to someone who is more "qualified."

.I tell you this because, in the normal sense, I was not trained to carry the responsibility of a Ceremonial Pipe. I had only my personal Pipe, which I used in my daily life to learn the ways to walk in balance. Its bowl was made of deer antler and its stem was made of sumac wood. At the time, I would not even think of having a Pipe made out of the sacred red or black stone of which most Ceremonial Pipes are made. I did not consider myself worthy, however, as you will see, the Pipe did.

I had been using my personal Pipe for several years, when I was given as a gift a very powerful and important Pipe, which had been created to do ceremony for the United Nations. It was carved in 1978 by Adam Fortunate Eagle, an *Anishinobie* (Chippewa) Elder, master Pipe Maker, and spiritual leader of the "Keepers of the Sacred Tradition of Pipe Making." The Pipe has a large turtle on the bowl, and four other little turtles, carved out of red pipestone, mounted on the cedar stem, all "following" the head turtle on the bowl. Adam presented the Pipe to delegates of the UN, and for seven years it was used to open many international negotiations and ceremonies. Even President Ronald Reagan took part in ceremony with it.

So here I am, suddenly in the care of this Pipe, which obviously should be with someone much more experienced in these ways. I happened to know of Adam, who had carved this Pipe for the UN. When I contacted him, to ask what I should do with it, he said I should come to a gathering being held in Pipestone, MN, the next week, and he would decide what should be done with it then.

This Pipe has a long story of its own, some of which I will relate later in this book. But since this is a history of the Black Thunder Bird Pipe, not the UN Turtle Pipe, I will just say that Adam decided the Pipe had chosen me to take care of it, and that I should carry that responsibility and learn the ways of the Ceremonial Pipe. He gave me a year to learn as much as I could from my own Elders, after which he would re-evaluate what should be done with that Pipe.

I am grateful to those who took me under their wings, and taught me so much in such a short amount of time, with such amazing patience. As the years have passed, I have continued to learn from the Pipe and the Elders it has brought me to. I believe I will continue to learn until the day

19

I pass over to the other side of existence.

I want to restate that, in the normal way, one is brought up from childhood with a Ceremonial Pipe like this, being an assistant to a Pipe holder for years until he or she are chosen *by the Pipe* as being ready for the responsibility. But this is the point: *It is the Pipe that decides who will care for. It is the confirmation of the Elders that helps to keep one's ego from misinterpreting that choice.*

So, there I was. I had had the responsibility of the UN Pipe for a few years when I received a phone call from a woman I knew, who wanted to know if I could help her evaluate some "artifacts" her late husband had collected. She was in need of money and wanted to sell his collection if it was worth anything. I agreed to help her, even though I felt like I was going to someone's house to tell them the market value of *my own* family's Bible, found on my family's old homestead.

She had a nice collection of arrowheads, spear points, and pottery, all old and worth a good deal, but what really caught my attention were several old Pipes she had in a box. Two of these were obviously taken from graves of the mound builders, and the others were wonderful examples of late 1800s-style Pipes. I told her she could get a good price for most of the collection, but it would not be wise to sell the Pipes. I advised her they should be returned to their original tribes or families, to be taken care of properly. She said she would think about it, but she really needed the money.

As I was getting ready to leave, she remembered one other Pipe she had, and asked if I wanted to see it. I said, "Of course." and she brought out a big, black stone Ceremonial Pipe with lead Thunderbird inlays on the bowl. This Pipe radiated power, and, if I understood its energy, displeasure. I was particularly drawn to it; after leaving I could not bear to think of this Pipe being sold to hang on someone's wall. The other Pipes seemed to be "asleep," for lack of a better description, but the Black Pipe was defiantly awake and not happy with the situation. I prayed about it over and over.

My Elders have said a Pipe goes wherever it wants to; it stays with whomever it chooses. They say a Pipe is more capable of getting to where it wants to be than we are. As things turned out, the widow ended up passing the Pipe on to me because of my helping her with the other items.

I was excited about the Pipe, and took it to show to a friend who is an Apache Medicine Woman. When she saw it, she would not even touch it, and told me I was not ready to use it, even though it had chosen to be in my care. So what did I do? I used it in a ceremony the next week. After all, I was responsible for the UN Pipe, why not this one also? (*First lesson from this Pipe...listen to your Elders*!!!) The ceremony went badly, and my ego was put in its place quite firmly, in front of over 50 people. It took years of sitting with this Pipe, caring for it and continuing to learn its ways, before I was released to use it in ceremony. Even now, it continues to be very demanding toward me as we travel together.

My relationship with the UN Pipe had been that of one with a gentle teacher - very nurturing. I soon found out the Black Pipe was not like this at all. This Pipe proved to be a very stern and harsh teacher! I did use it, and with astounding results, but it held me to account like never before! As I've learned to adjust to the Pipe's demands of me in my personal life, I have been blessed to be witness to many powerful and amazing "miracles" accomplished through it.

Now, I will continue with the actual history of the Thunder Pipe and what it has accomplished over the last few years. I wanted you to have a base from which to understand a very important fact: *The medicine (power) is held by the Pipe, not by the one who takes care of it.* There are other aspects about this but they are not appropriate for discussion in a book.

21

I was living in Colorado when I first received the Thunder Pipe, but have since moved to Montana. At that time, there had been a drought for more than seven years in both states.

One day, in the spring of 2002, I was on my way to a folk concert on the Flathead reservation in Montana when the Pipe, which I keep with me almost all the time, urged me to pull off the road and go into the National Bison Range. I felt it calling to me to pray for the young buffalo soon to be born. I did as I felt prompted, and as I prepared the Pipe for the ceremony, I was told to also pray specifically for the drought to be broken. I was lead to ask that it would rain *all summer* from the bison range in the south end of the valley, all the way to the northern tip of the Flathead Valley. Rain for the entire summer never happens there, even in a good year.

The very next day (twenty-four hours after the ceremony) it started raining, and continued throughout the entire summer. The rest of Montana was still in a drought, but the Mission and Flathead Valleys were so green that folks were complaining about how often they had to trim and mow. How quickly we forget!.

Later that summer forest fires broke out all over the still-dry mountains of Colorado. I still love the land there, and I determined to take the Pipe to Colorado and pray for rain. Now, I want to point out that the prayers for the Montana drought were instigated by the Pipe, but the prayers for Colorado where instigated by me. The differences in the results are important to note.

I traveled to Colorado, and started the Pipe ceremony at Turquoise Lake, near Leadville. Just before I was to start the ceremony, the Pipe was given a gift of a special bird wing, to be used in the ceremonies. To this day, it still travels with this Pipe. The other wing of that bird was used in ceremony by a Medicine Person, to "draw a line" where the fires were not to pass.

I intended to carry the loaded Pipe all the way to the south end of the San Luis Valley, several hundred miles, in order to cover as much of Colorado as possible with the rain I hoped would come. I followed the instructions given me for the ceremony, by striking the bowl of the Pipe into the water of the lake and pointing the stem towards the sky (clouds). It started raining 24 hours later, and the storm followed me for the next few days as I traveled across all parts of the state.

The thing to notice is in Montana the rain continued for the whole summer. In Colorado, however, it only rained wherever the Pipe was physically. As I traveled back home, it even rained across the desert of Utah, unfortunately lightning from the storm started some fires in the dry mountains there as well.

It was weird to be traveling in rain for almost a week, and to find out that it only rained where we had been, not anywhere else in the state. I wondered what the lesson was, and finally understood. I needed to let the Pipe initiate the ceremonies, not initiate the ceremonies myself.

I moved to the Bitterroot Valley in Montana the next summer, and the weather went back to a drought in the Flathead and Mission Valleys. We had some very bad forest fires in the Bitterroot, and I wanted to pray for rain with the Pipe. I did, and instead of rain I got this message from the Pipe: *it would not rain, as the fires were needed to restore balance in the area.* Not my idea of balance, but I have learned to trust the Thunder Beings, as they tend to have a broader perspective!

Ok, now we jump ahead to the spring of 2004. We had a ceremony, celebrating the *Awakening of Thunder*. During the ceremony, I jokingly said that if I were not doing the ceremony properly, everyone would know because I might not be alive four days later, inferring that if I were doing the ceremony improperly, I would get zapped by the Thunder Beings in four days. So, *guess what happened four days later?*

I was on a small plane taking off from the Seattle airport when the plane was hit by lightning! It fried some electronics in the cabin, lit up the whole inside of the passenger area, and scared the attendant so much she wet her uniform. No kidding! There I sat, wondering if the whole group of us was going to die because of my joking about the Sacred Pipe! Well, we didn't die. Instead, we had a forced landing, and I got a free night in a cheap hotel near the airport until a flight out the following day.

As I sat in my hotel room and pondered it all, the Thunders came to say it was not a punishment; it was to show everyone the reality of the ceremonies we were doing. I was told I needed to tell everyone who had attended the ceremony about this, and some other things that usually happen to folks after such a ceremony - things I had neglected to tell them.

As it turned out, several of them had indeed had those experiences, and were wondering what they meant. An example of these experiences is two ladies who attended and started their moon (menses) right after the ceremony, over a week early. Another example is of a person who became sick and couldn't sleep for three nights. This may have been because they did not heed my advice to refrain from using drugs or alcohol for three days prior to the ceremony. After I gave them the *complete* information that I should have given prior to the ceremony, these people were able to access what the Great Mystery was doing in and for them more completely, and were able to see the reality of the power of the Pipe. Good thing the Thunder Beings decided to make an example of my little "joke" about the four days.

As stated previously, the Bitterroot Valley had been plagued by huge forest fires for several years, all a result of a long-term drought. In the spring of 2004, the forestry and weather experts were predicting the worst year yet for forest fires. Of special concern were the fisheries of the Valley, due to the low snow pack in the mountains, and the extended drought. They said it would take two months of almost constant rain, as well as a late season snow pack build up - something that never happens - to get into a safe "zone." Things looked very bad, to say the least.

As is my custom, I was sitting holding the Pipe bundle in my lap one day and felt drawn to have a *Rain Requesting* ceremony. I also felt urged to ask Jason, a young Sundancer I knew, to join in the ceremony with me. I called him, and we arranged a time to pray down by the Bitterroot River. I knew one of the reasons for the ceremony and his attendance was to help him see the reality of the spiritual power of the Pipe. He has been exposed to many ceremonies through his experience with the *Sundance*; however, his upbringing caused him to cling to the security of the dogmatic aspect of ceremony. What he needed was to experience a ceremony where the answers to the prayers would truly *have* to be a miracle. As it turned out, the whole event was custom-designed to blow away anything he thought he knew about praying with the Pipe.

Jason met me down by the river along with Lora, my girlfriend at the time, and Connor, her three-year-old son. As we spread the blanket on the sand and got the Pipe out, Connor began running around playing, throwing sand, yelling, and generally being very disruptive to the seriousness of the ceremony. With all this distraction going on, it was obvious our ceremony would only have power if it was real, not something we drummed up with "just the right atmosphere."

We did the prayers and I created a pathway connection from the river water to the sky water with the Pipe. In our prayers I was directed to ask for a *full* season of good, gentle, "female" rain, as well as lots of extra snow on the mountains. The next day, exactly twenty-four hours later *to the minute (*I had learned to pay attention to the timing by then), I was about two blocks away from the river, sitting on a city bench with my friend Paul. I couldn't help but break out laughing, as we watched the rain come like a wall from the west and sweep across the valley.

I am writing this in October, 2004, and the ceremony was in May. We have had rain almost every day since then, as well as lots of late spring snow on the mountains. These supplied the rivers with the much-needed run-off for the fish and wildlife throughout the summer. Even the life-long residents of the Valley are saying they have never seen a year like this. We are now in the fall of the year, and continue to have daily rains.

There is a Shoshone-sponsored *Ghost Dance,* held every year just north of Missoula, MT, in Lubrecht Forest. Usually, it is a beautiful time of the year with crisp cool nights and fall colors throughout the forest. In the fall of 2004, it was cold and wet. I was asked by one of the spiritual leaders of the dance if I could do a *Splitting the Clouds* ceremony, so the dance would not be rained on.

I went into the ceremonial lodge on my property, and sat with the Thunder Pipe. I asked it if it would help the people at this dance. I felt its agreement, much as one married partner can sense what the other partner is feeling without a word. The instructions I received from the Pipe were that it would be improper to ask for the rain to stop, since it was through this Pipe the request for rain was made in the first place. Instead, it directed me to do an *Undoing* ceremony, wherein I was to "undo" the connection of the earth water with the sky water for just that area and for just three days. The dance grounds were to be marked for the spirits with a piece of lightning-struck wood, tied with specific colored ribbons.

One other thing I would like to mention is I often ask for someone I know and trust to join me in the ceremony, even if they are not able to physically be with me. In this case, I asked Tim and Hermi, a young Cherokee man and his wife who live in Austria, to pray with me at the designated time, (with appropriate adjustments made for the time difference). Tim received a vision during the ceremony, which explained the ceremony's outcome. When I talked to him the following day on the phone, he said he saw an osprey circling over the dance grounds, and there was water dripping off of its wings. As you will see, it was a perfect visual of what actually took place.

I arrived right before the *Ghost Dance* was to start, and was setting things up for the ceremony in an area to the west of the dance circle. The rain that had been falling steadily for several days had stopped just before I arrived. The sky was dark with low-lying clouds which looked as if they would start a deluge at any moment. I needed an assistant to help with the sage and sweet grass but everyone was busy getting things ready to start the dance. I asked if anyone could help me with the ceremony, and a young Blackfoot boy named Samson volunteered. I have to say I feel the main reason the Pipe wanted to do this ceremony had more to do with impacting this young man's life and less to do with the *Ghost Dance* itself.

After we finished the Pipe part of the ceremony, I had Samson pour water from a well located on the property onto a spot next to the dance circle's edge. I stuck the spike made from the lightening-struck wood into the ground, followed by the tip of the Thunder Pipe's bowl. I then did the required "undoing" part of the ceremony.

This done, we went to put the ashes left over from the smudge and Pipe into the sacred fire in the middle of the circle. As I put the ashes in the fire, a light rain started to drizzle. I was a bit perplexed that it would rain then when the Thunders had encouraged me to do this ceremony. I wondered if it might be just their way of putting my ego in

27

its place… again.

As I asked the Thunders why it was raining, they reminded me the outcome of the ceremony was their business, not mine, and they wanted the dancers to appreciate what they were doing for them. This was not exactly what I wanted to hear; I would have rather passed on a message like, "It will stop raining for exactly 36 hours," but I passed the information on anyway and left for home. This is an example of being available to do what the Pipe directs and not getting too hung up on the outcome.

The further I drove away from the area, the harder it poured! I live about two hours away from the dance grounds, and it rained almost non-stop at my house for the next three days. I was a bit worried about what was happening at the dance, but kept reminding myself that no matter what happened, it was as it should be. As it turned out, it rained throughout the whole weekend, *except* when the dancers came to the circle to dance. Every time they gathered, the rain stopped. It would rain all around the area, but the circle did not receive any. At the end of the dance, the man in charge of the fire pulled up the wooden spike I had placed in the ground. He followed my instructions, and put the spike in the fire to be burned. The smoke from it sent a message up to the Thunders that the dance was over and the "boundary" was dissolved. Needless to say, shortly afterward the rain started, and continued to pour. So you see, the vision of the osprey was correct. The "undoing" ceremony did protect the dancers, but water still dripped on them throughout the weekend.

Now I want to tell you about little Ashton. Ashton is a two-year-old boy in Kansas City, MO. He was born with serious heart defects, which the doctors said would kill him before he had lived but a few years. Although I have never met him, I heard about him through his grandfather, who is a member of the "Keepers" mentioned earlier. His grandfather,

Don, had requested prayers for him just before the annual gathering of the group in Pipestone at the end of July, 2004. On our trip from Montana to Pipestone, I felt the Pipe saying it wanted to intercede for Ashton. Now I would never think of giving someone false hope in a situation like this, but I have come to know that when the Pipe speaks this way, the outcome has always been dramatic and effective.

We arrived late at night so I did not get a chance to talk with Don. We heard he was leaving to return home early the next morning because Ashton was in the hospital again, and was not expected to live more than a few days. I thought I had missed the chance to offer to pray with Don using the Pipe. However, as I was getting a cup of coffee from another camp the next morning, Don came into the camp to say a last goodbye before hitting the road. I took him aside, and asked if he would like the Pipe to be used in a healing ceremony for Ashton. He readily agreed, and offered the Pipe an honor gift of tobacco.

There were about six of us who gathered in a small circle between two tipis to perform the ceremony. It was a powerful and moving experience for all involved. Don gave me a hug and jumped into his truck for the long drive home. The next morning, we got a phone call from Don. He was so excited. He said that when he arrived at his daughter's house, he was greeted at the door by a happy and energetic Ashton, who had been unexpectedly released from hospital because of a sudden and dramatic "recovery!"

We were all overjoyed by this news, and for the next few days, the whole gathering in Pipestone took on an air of excitement. There were several ceremonies scheduled to take place over the next few days, and with this answer to the Pipe, the enthusiasm among all those gathered was high. That evening the thunder clouds rolled in. Throughout the weekend, we were surrounded by amazing lightning shows and strange weather, but it only rained on us during one night that we were there.

This is not the end of Ashton's story. Over the next few weeks he had to go back to the hospital for tests and observation. To the amazement of all, his heart simply repaired itself. Yesterday I got a letter from Don, confirming the continued recovery of Ashton. I wonder what kind of special gift to the world this child will be. I do not doubt he will help change it into a better place, as so many other "miracle" babies have done before him.

About Valerie

In the process of writing this book, my editor, Valerie Barzetti, succumbed to a brain tumor. After two years of battling its progressive growth, using every available technique known to both modern and "alternative" medicine, she found herself partially paralyzed and in a wheel chair, with the doctors saying she had two weeks left to live. She could not walk, had difficulty with her speech, swallowing, and suffered double vision making it impossible to use her computer.

Because of her exposure to the Sacred Pipe through her work on this book, she was aware of the possibility of its assistance. She sent word to me that she wanted a Pipe ceremony. She offered the Black Thunder Bird Pipe some of her own home grown-tobacco, and we proceeded to conduct the ceremony in her back yard.

There is an important precedent here. In order for the Pipe to be of assistance, one usually has to request it. It is frustrating for one who cares for a Pipe to see loved ones and friends suffering from things that could be addressed by the medicine of a Pipe. The whole while Val worked on this book I watched her health decline. I knew that, in this case, I could not offer her a ceremony; the request had to come from her first.

In today's world, people seem to think they must have a huge crisis before they can ask for help in the form of ceremony. This is not so. Why wait until you have bronchitis to see a doctor when one would rather treat you for just a cold in the beginning?

Fortunately for Val, she decided the Pipe was here to help her, and she did not hesitate to call for its assistance. Immediately after the ceremony was completed, her double vision cleared and her speech was improved. I made a little bag out of the ashes from the ceremony, and told her to soak it in any tea she might be having for the next few days.

There was a big party thrown for her two days later, a kind of "go out in style" party. When I arrived, she was there in her wheel chair, telling me she felt much improved. Indeed, there were signs of improvement. Her speech was clear, as she greeted everyone who had gathered there, not to mention she ate a large plate of food from the potluck with no trouble swallowing! I found out she had been spending a lot of time at her computer, due to the improvement in her vision. At the end of the party, Val told me that after two years of trying everything, the Pipe was the only thing that had immediately brought improvement. She said it was too bad she had waited until "the end" before asking for its help. She asked if we could do another ceremony for her, and I agreed.

I arrived at her house the next afternoon, and we did another ceremony. I did not conduct it exactly as I did the first one. To have copied the first ceremony, even though it was quite successful, would have not worked. The spirit of the Pipe showed me a different way to pray, this time, keeping us in that vital flowing relationship with the Great Mystery, rather than trying to repeat yesterday's medicine. I took the ashes from the ceremony, mixed with some blue cornmeal blessed by a Hopi Elder, and, following the Pipe's directions, had her sleep with them under her pillow. A few days later she reported to me she was sleeping better and longer than she

31

had in several months.

The swelling of the tumor continued to grow, and Val knew it was just a matter of a day or two before the tumor would close her airway and suffocate her. I was privileged when Val asked me to conduct a *Passing Over* Pipe ceremony for her.

We sat at her dining room table, she in her wheel chair and the rest of us in chairs. I called on the Spirits to come and help her crossing be a good one. There were tears and laughter when she suddenly said she could feel the "hands" of a Spirit on her shoulders. She said she saw her Grandparents there, as well as a few other spirits. I had everyone leave the room, so I could explain to her what it is like on the other side. (This can only be done by someone who has been there.) She said she would miss us all so much but she was excited to go on with her new adventure. I asked her if she could, to send me a sign that her passing had gone well. It was to be in the form of a special kind of dragonfly - something only she and I knew.

The dragonfly, in the EXACT center of the mattress cover.

I went home with my heart full of her incredible love and courage. She went across in the early hours of the next morning. Her husband put the foam mattress cover she had been resting on outside to air out. It was a cold fall day, far too cold for insects to be out and about. When he went to retrieve it, that particular type of dragonfly was sitting right in the middle of it.

It is natural for us to project onto the Pipe what the answers of our request should be. In Val's case, we would have wanted to see a miraculous healing. Instead, she was given the gift of being able to fully participate in the celebration of her last days with those whom she loved, without the physical restrictions normally associated with that type of tumor.

Valerie Barzetti, smiling at life

You, Val, and I all have the *same* guarantee on life. We could be here for the next day or the next year, but the terminally ill have the same guarantee on life as a healthy person. This is one of the gifts of the Pipe: *to live in the now.* I have a bumper sticker on my truck that says, "I'd rather be *here now!"* I am sure Val agrees.

As you proceed through this book, I hope you will open your heart, as well as your mind, to realize the Pipe, this ancient gift from a most benevolent Great Mystery, can be a source of "uncommon assistance" in your life as well. Remember, if you are in need of help from the Sacred Pipe, you need to ask in the proper manner. All it takes is a small pinch of tobacco. It should be presented to the one who cares for the Pipe with your request for help. It is an honoring of the Pipe, not the one who cares for it. The meaning of this offering will be explained in a later chapter. Just know that it is real, because it works.

Chapter 2
The Native Mind

What is the Native Mind?

Before I continue, I need to say that to truly understand the Pipe and all it means, one must learn of it through what my Grandmother Lillie referred to as a "Native Mind." Conversely, it has been said by the Elders that to understand the Pipe *is* to understand the "Native Mind."

There is more than one way to perceive things. One way is not necessarily better than the other. It is like two men looking at a big tree from different sides. One sees a scar from a lightening strike; the other sees only a perfectly formed tree. They can argue all day about who has the correct perception of what the tree looks like. Both are correct, just seeing it from a different perspective. It seems as if none of us is able to see the whole "tree" on our own. This promotes healthy *interdependence*, if we are willing to put our ego in its proper place.

If I wanted to learn how to throw a boomerang, it only makes sense to learn it from the ones who use it daily, rather than to have it explained to me by a physics professor. The professor may be able tell me all kinds of facts about its design, etc., but he has probably never hunted with one, and couldn't tell me what it feels like to depend on one to provide food.

Likewise, understanding what the Pipe is has a lot to do with your perspective. In order to truly understand any part of Native American spirituality, it is helpful to perceive it through a Native viewpoint rather than that of a non-Native. Please keep in mind I am not saying the non-Native viewpoint is invalid. It is just a poor platform from which to understand what I am going to share with you about the Pipe. The concepts of the Native mind are different than those of the non-Native mind and somewhat difficult to describe, but I will try to through some examples.

Relationships

The first example of the different ways to see things is in regards to relatives. In Native traditions, there is what is called a "chosen relative" or a relative by choice. The Lakota call it your *"Hunka"* brother, father, sister, etc. To the Native mind, there is absolutely no difference between a blood relative and someone whom you have "adopted" through choice *and* ceremony.

I have a *"Hunka"* sister, who used to be my sister-in-law. When she and my biological brother got divorced, she and I decided our being relatives should not stop. We chose to continue to be brother and sister. In my mind she was just as related to me as my brother. Every aspect of how I think of her is truly as being my life-long blood sister.

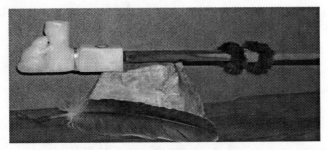

Beaver and tree effigy Pipe

Now this may seem easy to grasp, but here is what makes my mind a Native mind versus a non-Native mind. The concept that she is my "adopted" sister does not even *exist* in my mind. My every thought and action towards her is that of a physically related sister. As an example, when necessity bids we shed clothes, such as crossing a river or bathing while camping or rafting (things we do together often), I have no desire to look at her as a naked woman, but instead am adverse to the thought, just as one would never even think of looking at one's own blood sister in that way.

35

For the non-Native mind, the thought is not that way. Possibly it would say, "I must not look on her in that way because it is improper", but in the Native mind it is an automatic, *natural* reaction not to look. It actually is repulsive to look, just as it would be with my sister from the same physical mother. However, to the non-Native mind, there is the understanding that she *is* my sister, but always with the word "adopted" tagged to it.

Here is another example. I have a good friend who is a black man. He and I played softball on the same team, went out to dinner with our wives, etc. He eventually got a job working at the same company as me. One day I was talking to another employee who mentioned I was a friend of the new guy. He referred to him as "that black guy." I was shocked to realize I had not even been conscious of his skin color. Yes, every time I looked at him my eyes could see it, but that his skin was darker than mine never had been present in my thoughts. In the same way, my *Hunka* sister is just that, my sister.

Spirits

The Spirit of Eagle

So, now when you try to understand a concept like a Pipe has a Spirit just as you do, you can't grasp the concept until you think like a Native American. To the Native American way of thinking, *everything* has a Spirit, even inanimate objects.

36

Perhaps a better way to say it, *there is Spirit in everything.*

It is hard for those raised in a differing mindset to think that anything other than a two legged (human) has a spirit. They have been brought up believing that when their dog dies, it is just gone, it has no spirit. We who are Native know that when our dog dies, his Spirit leaves to be joined with the Great Mystery, just as our own spirit will. Many indigenous cultures bury their loved ones with their horse, their dog, their tools or weapons, as well as other things, to be with them on the other side. How can a horse or Pipe cross over to the spirit realm unless they have a spirit? It is obvious the physical horse stays with the physical body of the deceased, but if everything has a spirit, then it is not hard to understand the Spirit of the horse, as well as a Pipe or bow, goes with the person to the other side/dimension.

The Spirit of Bear

When we have a meal, we make up a "Spirit plate" for the Spirits and our ancestors to join us. Afterwards, the physical food on the plate remains but the food's spiritual essence has been consumed by our "guests." Another way to understand this is everything in this dimension has a counterpart in a different dimension, the one we call the realm of spirit.

Time

There is a term often used to describe an aspect of the Native American mind. It is also used to be critical of this mindset, viewing it as irresponsibility. The term is "Indian time." It is used when Native folks do not show up "on time" for something, like the start of a Pow Wow or for an appointment.

To the non-Native mind, everything is governed by time. There are calendars, clocks, etc. that *seem* to be a universal law, much like gravity. This is very real to the non-Native mind, but to the Native mind, there is only the constant "now."

For example, if you are on your way to a Pow Wow and meet someone whom you feel you should talk with, it is far more important to obey your intuition and spend "time" with this person. Yes, you may be late for the grand entry, but otherwise you would have missed whatever it was you were to receive or do by running into this person.

In the Native mind, it is far more important to be fully present in the moment, than to try to meet the demands of a future appointment, which has not even arrived yet, and might never arrive. To be worried about something two hours from now robs you of what is happening right now. The same goes about worrying about or living in the past. "Indian time" is actually a philosophy of living, not an excuse for irresponsibility. The bumper sticker on my truck that says, "I'd rather be here now!" in contrast to "I'd rather be fishing," I think, sums this thought up well.

Several years ago I was late for a class I was attending in Denver. As I rushed out of my hotel to get in my jeep, I heard a voice call out to me from the balcony above where I had parked. I looked up to see an old man with his morning cup of coffee, looking down at me. He asked where I had gotten the medicine wheel I had hanging from my Jeep's mirror and what did it represent. I explained I had made it and it represented the four cardinal directions.

As the conversation got more in depth about my spiritual path, I realized this man was a tribal Elder, and I was faced with a choice. Do I rush off so I could be on time for the class, or do I go with the flow and spend time with this man? My intuition told me this meeting was more than coincidence, so I chose to stay.

As things worked out, he eventually introduced himself to me. He said his name was Medicine Cloud. Later I found out he was a highly regarded Medicine Man. When I gave him some tobacco to show my respect for him as an Elder, he, in turn, gave me a beautiful healing feather. He said I had earned it. If I had allowed myself to be governed by "time" and schedule, I would have missed out on a wonderful conversation full of bits of wisdom, as well as the special feather!

Marriage and Divorce

To the non-Native mind, a marriage has to be "legal" to be real. To the Native mind, marriage is the state of your relationship. If the love and commitment are real, then the marriage is real. If there is no love relationship, there is no marriage, no matter what a piece of paper says. Most Native marriage ceremonies are very short and simple. Basically, they are an acknowledgment to the village that the two of you want to be considered as mates or partners from that point on.

Divorce is also based on actual relationship. If a couple decides to no longer be together, they simply make a statement, through recognized symbolism, that they are no longer partners. In the non-Native society, you are still married, even if you are living with another partner, until you have a document to prove the end of your previous relationship.

Land Ownership

To the non-Native mind, if you have a deed, you own some land. To the Native mind, it is impossible to own any part of the earth, as it is a living being, our Mother. To quote a wise man, "Can you sell your mother? Can you own the air?" The non-Native mind seems to be based on insecurity and mistrust, and has a need for "guarantees." It needs assurances on paper, in the form of deeds, licenses, copyrights, and contracts.

The Native mind assumes most folks walk with integrity (and they usually did), and security comes from the provision of a loving Creator, who has established a system which keeps all things in a state of balance. It is understood hardships are always followed by relief, and anything negative is only part of the positive in life.

No matter what our perception - Native or non-Native - it is a truth that the Great Mystery has put into place a great cycle of balance. The time is at hand (the _Age of the Pipe_) when, as we say, the hoop will turn, and all things will be brought back into balance.

So how do you get a Native mind? It isn't just a matter of genetics, but a way of thinking, in which you are either brought up or develop. It is when you _know_ there is a living Spirit in a Pipe, not just believe there is one. It takes trust to let your mind accept on faith the things presented here. I hope you can have the faith of a child and find that trust.

40

What Is the Pipe?

The Sacred Pipe of the North American Indians, commonly but erroneously referred to as the *Peace Pipe*, is far more than just an implement used in religious ceremonies. It is the center - the very heart - of most Native American spirituality. A Pipe is actually the physical dwelling of a spiritual helper, sent by the Great Mystery to aid humans to live in balance with themselves and the universe.

The way of the Pipe may not be for everyone, but it is not just for Native Americans alone anymore. In most legends about the origin of the Pipe, it is stated it was sent to bring this assistance to *all* the peoples of the Earth. Today, people from all ethnic backgrounds are finding the way of the Pipe to be the life path to which they have been called.

Much like the many other ways the Great Mystery has sent assistance to humans throughout history, the way of the Pipe was first given to a "chosen" people to learn from it. It then spreads its medicine/power amongst all of humankind to bring harmony. This wasn't done through proselytizing, or conquering and subjugating nations or individuals into accepting its truth. Instead its power and assistance have been spread around the world at a specific time in history, through individuals who have been called by the Great Mystery to have the responsibility of caring for a Pipe.

As Pipes are dispersed around the globe, their effect will be felt wherever they are located. Again, the way of the Pipe is not about converting people into believers. It is about Pipes being spread around the earth with those who have been chosen to care for them, eventually overlapping and covering the earth with the Pipe's power, influence, and harmony. You may not even be aware of it, but you may have been the recipient of blessings brought to your area by a Pipe already. If one is being used near you, its blessings rain down on everything around its location.

Where Did the Pipe Come From?

There are many legends about how the Pipe came to the different nations of Turtle Island (North America). These stories seem to be like the spokes of a wheel, all originating from one central hub. While there are many Pipes found all over the continent made of various materials, the origin of the red pipestone Pipe marked a new age of interaction between the Great Mystery and humans. The legend of how the first Pipes were created and sent throughout the continent is very logical in concept, and matches the many individual accounts of the arrival of the Pipe at the different tribes at different times.

Legends of the Pipe

There are several legends about how the first Pipe came to humans. The most common legend today is as follows:

In centuries past, there was a battle raging among several tribes on the site where we now quarry the red pipestone used in carving the bowls for our Pipes. It is said so many people were killed that their blood soaked deep into the ground and mixed with the earthly flesh of our Mother.

The Great Mystery saw the slaughter and was very sad that the people had forgotten how to live in peace with each other. He sent his messenger to stop the fighting. This powerful one appeared on the rock cliff overlooking the battle. He commanded the fighting to stop and all obeyed, so powerful was his voice and command. He then scooped up the mixture of blood and earth, and formed it into a Pipe bowl.

He made a stem out of the nearby hollow core branch of a sumac tree. He described to all present the meaning and medicine (power) of the red stone bowl and the wood stem. He described how the joining of the male (the stem) and female (the bowl) energies brought balance. He commanded that, from then on, no decisions concerning war or other important things were to be made without the equal balance of both male and female input, and that requests for guidance concerning these issues be made to the Great Mystery through the Pipe.

He went on to teach many other aspects of this sacred Pipe: how it would transform our prayers, first from a thought into physical form (through the tobacco), and then through the transforming energy of fire into the spiritual form (smoke), drifting our requests up to the attention of the Great Mystery. The Pipe acts as a kind of portal between the spiritual and physical worlds.

He then presented several Pipes to various Spiritual Beings who had come with the Great Messenger, assigning them to go to all the various nations on Turtle Island, and instructing them in its proper use. He said that when a Pipe was awakened for the first time by smoking it, he would send a Spirit helper to live in it to show the people the way of peace and harmony for their lives, both personally through an individual's Pipe, and corporately through the Ceremonial Pipe. This Spirit's residence in the Pipe is one reason we never say false or boastful things in the presence of a Pipe, for it will reveal the truth of what is said.

These Spiritual Beings then went into the four directions and presented the Pipes to many nations, at places considered sacred to them. One of these places was Bear Butte in South Dakota, where the Buffalo Calf Maiden gave it to the Lakota Nation. Another is a sacred lake in the Smoky Mountains, where a great serpent presented it to Red Arrow Woman of the Cherokee.

There are many descriptions of the various Spiritual Beings who brought the gift of the Sacred Pipe to the nations. It is interesting that the one who brought the Pipe to the people was almost always a woman. In most of the legends, it is said the Pipe was to come first to the nation who has the legend, but that the end results of its teachings was the joining of all nations of the earth into one family. One of the seven sacred ceremonies of the Pipe given to the Lakota is the "making of relatives" - the joining of non-blood-related people or tribes into a relationship as strong as any blood relationship (this is the *Hunka* ceremony mentioned previously).

Female and Male Pipes

As with all things of this world, Pipes come with the aspects of both male and female energies/attributes. This is reflected by the style of some modern versions of Pipes that began to appear around the time of the Caucasian invasion of Native

American lands. The most common image of a Sacred Pipe is the "T-style" Pipe of the Plains Peoples. It is generally accepted that a "T-style" Pipe is a male Pipe and an "L-style (elbow) Pipe is female. This is often the case but not always. Again, one must have a living relationship with the Pipe to know what "energy" it has. Some Pipes even have both energies in them. It is interesting to note that if you put a "T" Pipe and an "L" Pipe together they form the cross of the four directions of the medicine wheel.

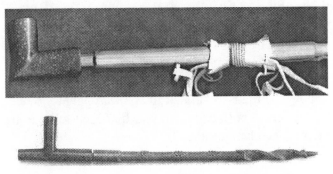

Top: "Elbow-Style" Pipe; Bottom: "T" Style Pipe

It is thought the "T" Pipes came into existence to signify the shift from the matriarchal social structure of the Native people to a male-dominated society. Although temporary, this shift to the patriarchal social structure was necessary, due to the change in lifestyle of the Native peoples. Previously, tribes had taken a stand-and-defend approach to intrusion by other tribes; however, the invasion of the Europeans forced the Native peoples to adopt a much more nomadic lifestyle as they were driven from their homelands. A village had to be able to react immediately to threat from the white soldiers by fleeing their homes

This new way of "living" was further amplified by the white explorers' unwillingness to acknowledge the clan mothers, always asking to speak to the village "Chief". Again, this is an example of the non-Native mind's inability to grasp the concepts of the Native mind.

The male, defensive time is now over. Now, the shift is towards honoring *both* the matriarchal and the patriarchal, which was, after all, the original intent of the gift of the Pipe. The trend among Pipe makers today reflects this, through the carving of more universal-style Pipes, sometimes in the form of the medicine wheel. I see this as the beginning of the restoration of the intended purpose of the Pipe, which is to unify and restore the balance of both male and female, race to race, etc. The styles of Pipes are a reflection of the condition of the Native American people. When the "L-style" Pipe was predominant, the society was more matriarchal. Then, as the society shifted to more patriarchal, the "T-style" became prominent. Now, Pipes like the medicine wheel Pipe reflect the trend towards a society where both the matriarchal and the patriarchal are joined into interdependence, both equal, and both needed for leading the people into the changes ahead.

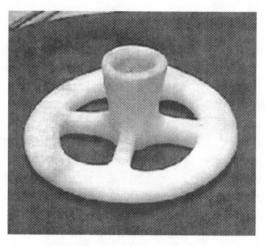

Alabaster Medicine Wheel Pipe

46

Chapter 3
The Way of the Pipe

Unity in Diversity

Just as there are many different denominations in Christianity, there are many different ways of walking with the Pipe. If one says their way is the only true way to walk with it, it causes the same kind of destructive division that plagues the Christian religion today. Folks who are supposed to be from the same spiritual family even go so far in their self-righteous attitudes as to kill each other!

If the way of the Pipe is approached in a religious manner instead of a spiritual one, the same thing can occur. I know of a Lakota man who interrupted a Muskogee Pipe ceremony and dumped the tobacco - the prayers - out of the Pipe and onto the ground. He did this because the Pipe had not been filled in *his* way. This would be unthinkable for anyone who has a living relationship with the Pipe. Much to the credit of the Muskogee, he said nothing but took the dismantled Pipe to his lodge, and grieved the rest of the day over how it, not he, had been treated.

I have a group of dear friends, a *Hunka* family, in central Colorado. We used to get together in a lodge behind one of the men's houses regularly to talk, pray, and support each other. However, we had a small problem in the beginning, as there were four Pipe holders among us. One was Lakota, one Muskogee, one Cherokee and one Onondaga! When we decided to load the Pipes, we all did so differently. The first time there was singing and praying and all kinds of commotion. As we continued to go through our individual ceremonies, a beautiful chorus emerged. There was singing in the background, prayers offered in turn, and a kind of choreographed spirit dance took place.

The Pipes brought a unity out of our diversity, which came

47

closer to what I feel the ceremony is really supposed to be like. This was a small miracle, as we all had tried for years to get together, but our different backgrounds (egos?) kept getting in the way. After the communal Pipe ceremony, we were able to put aside our different ways, and focus on our similarities. It was one of the most wonderful groups I have had the privilege to be associated with.

Personal and Ceremonial Pipes

It is important to understand there is a difference between having a personal Pipe and being the caretaker of a Ceremonial Pipe. It takes a lifetime of personal dedication and sacrifice to be a "carrier" (caretaker) of a Ceremonial Pipe, and the repercussions from the spiritual realm for improperly caring for such a Pipe can be very harsh. No one should take on these responsibilities or do public ceremony with such a Pipe unless they have learned the ways of this disciplined walk from another Ceremonial Pipe holder.

The physical size of the Ceremonial Pipe is often, but not always, longer or bigger than a typical personal Pipe. What truly designates a Pipe as a Ceremonial Pipe is based on the medicine of the Spirit that resides in the Pipe, as well as how and by whom the Pipe was presented to the one who is being entrusted with its care. There is usually a consensus of several Tribal Elders about it being placed in someone's care.

Top: Personal Turtle Pipe
Bottom: Ceremonial Bear Clan Pipe

48

The purpose of this book, however, is to assist you in your relationship with a personal Pipe. I cannot even begin to imagine the years of mastering the things one must know, in order to carry out the responsibility of a Ceremonial Pipe, could ever be conveyed in written form.

The personal Pipe is just as sacred and powerful as a Ceremonial Pipe, but it is somewhat more forgiving to the person who lives with it. Its purpose is to assist the individual, instead of the people in general. Therefore, the responsibility of the individual who cares for it is less than someone who is responsible for an entire tribe or nation.

One *never* owns a Pipe, for after it has been "awakened" through ceremony, it becomes the physical dwelling of a Spiritual Helper (just as our physical bodies house our Spirit). Once you take up a Pipe, you enter into a wonderful and demanding relationship, which can lead you to the highest expression of yourself. It is interesting to see how the Great Mystery has created the interdependence of all things. Just as we need the oxygen created by trees to live, so the trees need the carbon dioxide we create. So it is with the Pipe. We need its direction and intervention; it needs us to care for it and provide the ceremonies through which it does its work.

For the non-Native mind, I like to compare it to the relationship between a knight of the Middle Ages and his squire. The knight is like a Pipe; he is the one who does all the fighting and liberating, the one who has and is the power. The squire is like the one who cares for a Pipe. He takes care of all the physical needs of the knight, polishes the armor, announces his arrival, sees to the proper transportation, etc. You become a servant to the Pipe, just as the squire serves the knight, and just as a knight provides for his squire, the Pipe provides for its human caretaker.

The Spirit which dwells in the Pipe that comes into your life can come in many forms - animal, angel, ancestor, etc -

whatever form you personally can accept and relate to. This Spirit will teach you how to care for the Pipe, its new home, and in doing so, teach you how to care for yourself and others. For example, you will learn what kind of mixture to smoke in it, and how it wants to be wrapped and transported. All of these lessons will have a spiritual application, as well as a physical one. I have learned how to better care for my own body because of how I have been taught to take care of the Pipe (body) of my Spiritual guide. An "unhealthy" Pipe can't accomplish as much as a "healthy" one, just as with a healthy versus unhealthy person.

Tobacco

Just as there are many different kinds of Pipes, there are many different mixtures of herbs that can be gathered and smoked. The mixture, as well as the way the Pipe was created, will often determine the main area of influence it has, or its "medicine."

Some popular ingredients that are used for smoking in a Pipe are yarrow, *yerba santa*, deer's tongue, mint, dried flowers, bearberry (also called *Kinnikinnik*), the inner bark of red willow, and, of course, tobacco. Mullein, which is not native to North America, has been used ever since its introduction, to help mellow the harshness of many mixtures. In the northern areas, bearberry leaves were often used alone. Among the plains tribes, *ChinChasha* (red willow) was often the only ingredient. Tobacco itself was cultivated by many tribes, but due to its strength and scarcity, was seldom used alone. The modern strains of tobacco are much milder than the original plants, and most commercial blends have additives that, in my experience, have led me to seek out only organically grown tobacco.

When gathering these herbs, I try to sense which plants are willing to offer up their lives, to be part of the mixture that will be used in ceremony. I find they actually seem eager to be of assistance, as if it is their destiny. How do you talk

50

with a plant? It is done with the language of the heart. All of creation will respond to you, if you speak from your heart; it seems only humans have forgotten how to hear this language.

When I gather red willow bark, I only take it from the south side of the tree. This is to provide a better healing of the cut. I also only take the bark of the red willow during the months when the "thunder sleeps" (the months of winter, the months when thunder is not usually heard). The willows are dormant at that time, and the cutting and scraping is less traumatic to them then. I always leave an offering, in respect for their sacrifice. Sometimes this is a small bit of my person (such as some of my hair), but I always offer at least some tobacco or cornmeal, in return for the gift of the bark.

I might add here that drugs such as marijuana and peyote are *not* included in these mixtures. It is a general rule that you should not smoke the Sacred Pipe anywhere from one to four days within partaking of drugs or alcohol. To do so invites more trouble than it is worth! You need to be of clear mind and body to receive the blessings the Pipe will bring to you.

Kinnikinnik or Bearberry

51

Chapter 4
The Parts of the Pipe

Hole drilled for tobbaco mix

Hole drilled for stem

The Pipe Bowl

The bowl, called the *Chanupa* in Lakota, is the female aspect of a Pipe. Pipes can be carved out of many different kinds of stone, including soapstone, greenstone and alabaster, but the most common today are the red pipestone (Catlinite) and the black pipestone (Steatite) from Canada. Both are sacred to us, and are available through the "Keepers" organization mentioned at the end of this book. One word of caution here: Alabaster makes a beautiful Pipe, but tends to crumble from the heat of smoking. The town of Pipestone, Minnesota is the location of the sacred quarries where we gather the red pipestone used to create the bowl of many of our Pipes, as well as the site of the legend previously described.

Under the supervision of the U.S. government *and* tribal authorities, the stone can only be harvested in the old traditional way, by registered Native Americans. No power tools are used, and it is grueling work to break up the 10-to-15-feet-thick layer of hard Quartzite rock that covers the thin layer of pipestone beneath it. Today, many of those who remove the stone from the quarries give offerings back to Mother Earth before removing her "skin" to retrieve the precious layer of sacred stone. Sometimes we give offerings of our own flesh. As you can see, we do not take lightly so great a gift from our Earth Mother, and the Great Spirit.

*Travis Erickson, fourth generation Lakota quarrier, preparing to sing a
blessing song at the quarry*

The Pipe Stem

The Pipe stem, called the *Calumet* in Lakota, is the male aspect of a Pipe. Because both the stem and the bowl of the Pipe are sacred and have their own individual power, both are due great respect. By the divine design of the Great Mystery, it is only when the two aspects are brought together in balance that they can find their fullest ability to be of service to the inhabitants of this earth. This is another reflection of how it is with us Two Leggeds. It is only when we attain a balance of both our female and male sides that we can be the fullest expression of whatever it is we have been called to do. This applies to us personally, as a people or nation, and as a race as well.

It is the stem that is usually adorned with representations of the personal medicine of the one who cares for the Pipe. My personal Pipe stem has meaningful feathers, carved totems, and beadwork that represent my personal spiritual "helpers." The United Nations Turtle Pipe, which I mentioned earlier, has nothing personal on its stem. It would be hindered in its work if I put my personal, limited "medicine" on it. Also, it would seem logical from its history that this Pipe will be passed on to another caretaker when the time is right, possibly within a few more years. Many times when a Pipe is passed on or given as a gift, it will have a new stem with it, to be "personalized" by the new caretaker. The old stem is then wrapped in sage and kept on the family altar or, if the original caretaker has passed away, it is buried with them.

Old Pipes

I am often asked if it is proper to display old Pipes in museums and private collections, or to purchase a used Pipe. The answer is *no*. The purchase of an awakened Pipe is discussed in a later chapter. For now, it is important to understand the idea that a Pipe can be owned is not of the Native mind. So, you can see that as long as Pipes are thought of as property and artifacts, it will never be understood why we feel as we do about such displays.

To put the Pipe together is to start the ceremony, and it "teases" the Spirits. Things of the Spirit world are not based on our logic; they happen according to a different set of "natural" laws. If you put a Pipe together, you start a chain of events that cannot be stopped, regardless of whether you do the rest of the ceremony or not. The ceremony has been designed to give a constructive channel or direction for the power set in motion by assembling a Pipe. If that power is not properly directed, it can cause things to go awry.

If the old Pipes are to be displayed in spite of our views about it, at least the bowls should be smudged and plugged with sage by an Elder, and the stem separated from the bowl. I offer to make replicas of old Pipes, for just the cost of the materials, for any collector or museum who is willing to return the original Pipe to its proper tribe or family. There is always an exception to every rule, and I have been told by Elders it is acceptable to have a Pipe that has been "retired," through proper ceremony, on a family altar or some other place of honor. Pipes are retired from service for many reasons, such as the bowl developing a crack, etc.

To illustrate how important it is to show proper respect for the Pipe, I will mention here a little more of the story of the Black Thunder Bird Pipe from the beginning of this book. As you recall, I was shown a box with some old Pipes in it, which were part of a widow's deceased husband's collection of artifacts. She was in need of money, and wanted to sell the collection.

As was previously mentioned, I told her that to sell some of the things would be fine, but warned her, as gently as I could, not to sell the Pipes. I suggested she return them to the respective tribes of origin. I mentioned how sad it was that one Pipe, which had both the stem and bowl made entirely out of red Pipestone, had been broken into several pieces. She responded by telling me the story of how it happened. As she told it to me, I had to bite my lip to keep from telling her what I felt was the cause of her husband's death.

It seems they had just moved into a new house, and he was anxious to put the artifacts out on display. He decided to hang the Pipes on the wall as decorations. As he began to pound a nail into the wall, the hammer slipped out of his hand, landing on the Pipe in question, and broke the stem into three pieces. She said he was very angry, because it had cost him thousands of dollars. She then mentioned he had a heart attack a few days later, at the age of 41. I believe in the many years he had spent collecting the artifacts, he was made aware of the sacred nature of the Pipes he had in his care, and from my own experience with the Pipe, I would think that it probably had warned him several times about its care, or lack thereof.

Just because he didn't believe in the information, as is evident from his treatment of them, it did not exempt him from the consequences of his actions. However, there was no reason to add to her grief by telling her what I understood. As I said in the beginning of this book, "The misuse or even the lack of proper care of the Pipe can cause many severe and detrimental things to happen, just as the proper use and care can lead you to becoming the highest expression of the unique wonder you were created to be."

I want to mention one more thing about displaying a Pipe. There has recently been added a new category, "Pipes as sculpture," to the list of Native art forms judged by SWAIA (Southwestern Association of Indian Artists) at the annual Indian Market held in Santa Fe, New Mexico. It is understood, however, that these Pipes will never be used in ceremony. Most have the stems permanently attached to the bowl or the hole sealed in the bowl, so they may never be "awakened."

Pictured below is an example of a Pipe that was being carved as a Ceremonial Pipe, but developed a crack, making it unusable in ceremony. I completed it without the air hole, and made a stand for it of antler and mountain mahogany. Note the unusual coloring of the stone bowl.

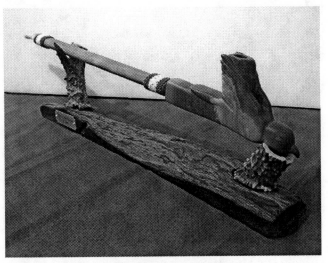

"Flight of the Phoenix"
A non-functional Pipe for display

Chapter 5
Purpose and Care of the Pipe

The Purpose of the Pipe

As stated before, the work of the Pipe is to help us walk in harmony with all of creation. Just as each individual human has special gifts, talents, or callings in their life, so each Pipe has a special "medicine" so it can do its part in restoring us all to the great unity. There are Pipes created for healing, to influence the weather, help bring visions, etc. These are usually Ceremonial Pipes.

The arrows of the Ayvdaqualosgv, {Thunders} protectors of the Pipe

Most personal Pipes have a more general medicine of being a teacher, protector, and intercessor for the one it dwells with, helping him or her deal with the day-to-day issues of life and restoring the caregiver to *"Hozzro,"* the Dineh word for harmony or balance.

An example of a Pipe having a special purpose or influence is the United Nations Turtle Pipe I mentioned in the beginning of this book. In the teachings of the *Anishinobie,* there are seven totemic beings that represent the seven levels or steps to a successful relationship. The very first one is the turtle. It represents truth, and is considered the foundation on which all other aspects of a relationship are constructed. The truth it represents is total, nothing hidden. Obviously, if a relationship, be it between individuals or between nations, is built on such truth, it will have a strength that will withstand all kinds of pressure.

This Pipe has a turtle carved on the bowl, with four smaller pipestone turtles mounted on the long, flat, cedar stem. The big turtle on the bowl of this Pipe represents the United States, (referred to by the *Anishinobie* as "Turtle Island"), and is a reminder that the US is to set an example of truth which the other turtles (i.e. other nations) are to follow, if we are to achieve true and lasting peace. As mentioned previously, this Pipe was used at the UN for seven years. It then disappeared for seven more years, until it was discovered by an aid to the UN, in a box in the basement of the UN building. He sent it to a retired UN representative of the United States, Jean Fitzpatrick. Ms. Fitzpatrick sent it to a Tibetan Lama, who, for the next seven years, kept it on an altar in his Ashram. He passed it on to me five years ago. You have already read that part of this Pipe's story.

The "medicine" of this particular Pipe is to reveal truth, and, thus, create a firm foundation for unity of nations, as well as of individuals. To illustrate this, I will tell you of a dramatic "miracle" performed by the Pipe, when it revealed truth to a group located near Sacramento, California.

It started with the leader of the group, who claimed to have been trained in Native American "shamanism" (there is no such thing), contacting me about doing a Pipe ceremony to bless some land the group had just purchased. They offered to fly me out there from Colorado, and cover all my meals and lodging. I asked the Pipe if it would go, and got a solid "yes." I should point out that I thought the Pipe's agreeing to go to this group was also its condoning of their "authenticity." I had my doubts, but thought if the Pipe said it was okay, they must be okay.

When I arrived at the leader's house, I was surprised to see the group was obviously some kind of cult. The woman who was the leader was a dominating force, who had built the cult around a mishmash of teachings which included witchcraft, Native beliefs, and a twisted version of Alcoholics Anonymous teachings. She had a firm control of all of her followers, and, through fear and guilt, manipulated their every move. Normally, I would have left immediately, but I knew the Pipe had agreed to go to these people, so I kept my mouth shut, and determined to just go with the flow.

The first night we had a "fire ceremony." It was full of lots of "mystical" and very theatrical use of blankets, tobacco, the fire, and an owl tail fan. The leader called on the Spirit of Owl to come and join us. She was very dramatic when she announced she felt the arrival of Owl, much to the trembling fear of the others in the group. I am not sure what she had told them Owl represented, but it was obviously something to fear, as if they would die if they made even the smallest mistake.

They passed the tail feather fan around the circle and everyone had to confess some terrible "sin" they had committed the previous week. After that was finished, the leader introduced me as a "shaman" and Pipe "carrier." I greeted them simply, and said I was going to load the Pipe and pray. You could have heard a pin drop. Apparently, the leader had not planned on this, telling them that only she would be doing ceremony with me privately. Well, I had already started and she couldn't intervene, for fear of looking bad in front of her followers.

As I said, the medicine of this Pipe is to reveal truth, in order for people to find unity. Just before I lit the Pipe, I said something that, to this day, I know came from the Pipe and not me. I said, "It is one thing to call on the Spirit of Owl and then tell others you "feel" its arrival. But if what they are doing is real, then one would expect *real* owls to show up." I then, half jokingly, called out, "I call on the Spirit of Owl to come join us!" Well, you guessed it. Immediately, two screech owls came out of the night, and began to swoop just above the heads of the group. They called and screeched, and pretty much scared the bejesus out of everyone! I noticed they were grabbing little moths as they dive-bombed the air just above the fire, where the moths had congregated.

To top off the evening, as I held the Pipe I heard it say, "There is going to be an earthquake tonight." I told everyone this, and sure enough, around 3 a.m., the area was rocked by an earthquake! Needless to say, the group paid very close attention to me for the rest of the weekend.

I spoke on several occasions about independent spirituality, that they already knew everything they needed to know, they just needed to have someone remind them of it. I addressed, as gently as I could, the problems with "medicine folks" leading people astray for personal profit and gratification. The leader finally got me on a plane a day early, to get rid of me, but I found out the group split shortly after our visit. Half of the group left to find their own individual path and half stayed, unable to break away from her manipulative hold.

About a week after I had returned home, I was instructed by the Pipe to send a message to the woman who led the group. It was basically a warning to stop her manipulations and walk a good path. If she did, she would be blessed, but if she did not heed the warning of the Pipe, things would go badly for her. She chose not to turn from her ways and shortly after she was responsible for the death of two young people in a fraudulently-run sweat lodge. This brought in the authorities, as well as the outrage of the Native community. Her darkness had been brought out into the national spotlight; the truth was revealed.

To this day, the UN Turtle Pipe is called upon to lift the prayers of multi-national/racial groups, in hopes of peace around the world. It has been responsible for several groups "splitting," due to the revealed truth about how they were operating. One thing of interest is that the mix used by this Pipe is made of seven herbs, representing the seven nations of the world (stone nation, the two leggeds, the four leggeds, the winged ones, the swimmers, the crawlers, and plant nations). The unity we are destined for is with *all* our relations, all the children of Creation, not just humans.

Care of the Pipe

A Pipe needs to be properly cared for, not only in the physical realm, but spiritually as well. Just as a Pipe will become plugged up with resins from smoking it, so it can become blocked spiritually speaking. Two things to be aware of, which can affect the performance of a Pipe, are improper storage and handling, and bringing it into public view for purposes other than ceremony.

Most of all, Pipes should be protected from coming into contact with a woman on her moon (menses), since this is when her personal medicine is at its peak power. Her medicine can actually overpower the medicine of the Pipe, as well as other sacred things. This has nothing to do with the Judeo-Christian idea that a woman is "unclean" during her cycle. It is based on the understanding that she is in the time of her greatest power, the renewing of her power to create life. I have witnessed some amazing things accomplished by women on their moon doing sacred ceremony, but again ladies, this is not to be tried without proper understanding.

Just coming near a woman on her moon can hurt the most powerful Pipes. It should also be noted that whatever happens to the Pipe happens to the one caring for it. I had a personal experience with this situation, when a friend of mine, who was on her moon, accidentally came into a circle where we were passing the Pipe. I had not properly informed everyone of this protocol (not mixing moon medicine with the Pipe). What happened to me is a good example of why you need to follow protocol, even if it may not make sense to you at the time.

The ceremony we were having was during a total eclipse of the full moon, which possibly amplified the effects of the situation. I was standing in the circle as the Pipe was being passed clockwise, when my friend, the one on her moon, walked up directly behind the one holding it. Instantly, I felt as if a hand were crushing the breath out of my lungs, and at the same moment, the woman staggered back, as if an invisible hand shoved her away from the Pipe. I could barely speak, but said, "Get her away from the Pipe." I do not know where the words came from, as my back was turned to where she had entered, and I had no idea what was happening. Thankfully, no one was hurt, but we all learned a powerful lesson in respecting tradition.

Part of the protection for a Pipe is to keep it in a leather Pipe bag made especially for it. This bag will be discussed more fully, under "Pipe accessories" later.

Simple Pipe Bag

It is considered proper to hold a Pipe, whether assembled or in the bag, in the crook of your left arm, the one closest to your heart, much as one would hold an infant, cradling and protecting it as something very fragile. Also kept in the bag are kept a pouch of smoking mix, a tamper stick for keeping the mix burning, various medicine objects, and herbs such as sage, cedar and sweet grass.

There is an herb which is known to help protect the Pipe from things that could interfere with its medicine. It is called Bear Root. I try to always have some handy and usually wrap it with the bowl of the Pipe in a piece of leather or cloth separate from the stem.

Sundance sage (long leaf sage) is often tied to the stem, as a way of protecting it. The idea of wrapping the stem and bowl separately is not only to cushion the objects in the bag, but also to keep them covered from view until they are about to be used.

When filling a Pipe, there are many different ways to hold or position it, depending on the differing tribal traditions, as well as taking into account the particular Pipe's own preference. In my tradition, one holds the Pipe bowl in your left hand, with the stem either over your left shoulder or in the crook of your left arm. Pinches of your mix are then placed into the bowl with the right hand. Even though this is the way I was shown to do the loading, I care for a Pipe whose preference is to be laid on the ground with the stem pointing north during this part of the ceremony. So you see, the truly "correct" way to do anything in regards to the Pipe is determined by each individual Pipe itself.

There are many age-old traditions about how to care for a Pipe. These things have been passed down through the generations because they are real and they work. I have found if I first honor a tradition for that tradition's sake, it will lead to an understanding of it. In the words of the Lakota Holy Man, Nicolas Black Elk, *"The power of a ceremony is in the understanding of it.*" Without fail, I have found that, by honoring a tradition, the understanding of it, and thus the power of it, always follows.

Never bring a Pipe out of its wrappings unless intending to do ceremony with it. To do so not only invites attention to it from possible unwanted persons or energies, but as mentioned previously, it also "teases" the Spirits. If I am taking the Pipe out of its bundle to clean it, I always smudge it and offer some tobacco or mix to its Spirit. I explain I am going to clean the Pipe, so the Spirit will understand how to direct its power. I find the Pipe seems to "relax," for want of a better word.

Anishinobie Pipe, sumac stem

Salish Pipe holder

Chapter 6
How to Use the Pipe

General Protocol
Concerning Ceremonies and Elders

As mentioned before, there are traditions that have been developed over the centuries that have proven effective even though their reasoning seems clouded to the non-Native mind. Things such as offering tobacco or cornmeal (pollen) in prayer or to an Elder do not seem to have any real value in today's world. Once again, as Black Elk said, "the power of a ceremony is in the understanding of it." I will give you a basis of understanding of the protocol we follow, in order to help you access the power of them. Please keep in mind these understandings are just a starting point. They are from my limited experience, and should serve as a *basis* for your spiritual experience, not as a rule or a confined way of thinking.

Explaining the Ceremony

One of the most basic things done by Native peoples of this continent is the showing of respect and honor through the offering of tobacco. This is done to honor Elders, Spirits, and those who serve the people through healing and teaching, etc.

67

The reason tobacco is considered a gift of honor is because of what it represents, as much as what it is. In the old days, tobacco was a rare and sacred herb. It was used both in ceremony and for its curative properties. It used to be a very different plant, just as corn was, before genetic engineering and hybrids completely changed them. Originally, the fruit of both corn and tobacco was much smaller and far more concentrated. Nowadays, they have been bred into higher-yielding plants, but are much weaker in their medicine and nutrients. The original tobacco was so strong it would kill you, or at least make you very ill, if taken in the quantities used today. In traditional Pipe mixtures, it was proportionately a very small component, compared to the other things used in the mix.

So, when you offered a pinch of tobacco in those days, it meant a sacrifice of a precious herb. Today, many have not understood the medicine of tobacco and so think that offering more is better. Not so. I have received huge tubs of commercial tobacco that had less meaning than a small tobacco tie given with the right intention and understanding of its spiritual value. I will describe tobacco (prayer) ties a little later in this section, but know they need only contain a small pinch of tobacco to have great medicine.

When you offer an Elder some tobacco, say as a prelude to asking advice, it is just as appropriate to give a small pouch as to give a whole tub. As a matter of fact, to give the tub may reveal you give the gift from an inaccurate understanding of why you do it. Also, when you give an offering of tobacco to the Spirits, Mother Earth or the Great Mystery, it isn't the size of the offering; rather it is the intent that matters. It was easier for me to understand why I offer tobacco to the Spirits when I thought of them as physical Elders. It is the Spirit of the tobacco that they receive, just as it is the Spirit of the food offered on the Spirit plate during a feast.

Gifts and Honors

Depending on the circumstances, there are different gifts to show honor other than tobacco. When you give a gift, it should be given with "no strings" attached. Often, we give something in order to gain some kind of recognition from the recipient. We want to be recognized or appreciated. This is not a proper mind set for spiritual giving. If the one you give it to turns immediately to another and gives it to them, your reaction will let you know if you have given it in the right way. If you are offended or feel like your gift wasn't valued, you have not given it with a right attitude. If you understand that the gift, once given, is no longer attached to you, you will not be offended, but blessed, to see the one you gave it to felt it was special enough to be passed on as a gift to another person they respect.

The way I was shown to give a gift (but this is only the way I was shown), was to honor the four directions while giving it. The four directions represent many things, but when giving someone a gift, they represent the following:

❖ *the East represents the way of the newborn and young child,*

❖ *the South represents the way of the child/adolescent,*

❖ *the West represents the way of the adult life,*

❖ *the North represents the way of the Elder.*

When you hand the gift to someone, you place it into their hands four times, once for each direction, thus honoring the entire life cycle of the recipient. Usually you hand it to them from your right hand into their left.

Some appropriate gifts are as follows:

❖ *When asking advice or assistance from an Elder, offer tobacco or corn meal. The medicine of tobacco is often associated with the aspects of the male; the medicine of the cornmeal is that of the female.*

❖ *To ask for special assistance from the spirit world*

> through a Medicine person, present a loaded Pipe to
> be smoked with them,

- ❖ *To honor an Elder woman, offer a star quilt or wool blanket,*
- ❖ *To honor an Elder man, present a jacket, sweater or gloves.*
- ❖ *Other gifts that show honor could be feathers, special rocks or wood, perhaps carved, or some bead work, especially if you created it.*

Remember, as with any gift, always think of what would be meaningful to the recipient - don't get hung up on dogmatic rules. I have heard of Elders who, when they passed away, left behind a closet full of gift blankets, but their gas tanks and cupboards were empty.

It is important to understand that when you come to someone who cares for a Pipe, the gift you bring is to the Pipe, rather than to the one carrying it. Appropriate gifts for a Pipe are items it uses, such as tobacco. However, since most Pipes have their own special mix, it is often more thoughtful to bring sweet grass, sage, bear root, cedar, a Pipe tamper, or bags and pouches to hold the many things used with the Pipe.

I remember one time when a wonderful Lakota Elder was coming to Wyoming to run a sweat lodge for my friends. I wanted to give him something that would not only show my respect, but which he would be delighted to have as well. I prayed and asked for guidance, and the Spirits showed me a picture in my mind of a plaid wool shirt/jacket I had in my closet. It was a brand new Pendleton (still had the tags on it), with leather patches on the elbows.

I took it to the sweat, and when I gave it to the Elder, he was delighted! He said he loved plaid and really liked the elbow patches, said they were real fancy. I am not saying my gift was better than a pouch of tobacco, but the point I want to make is it is often better to follow your intuition about what would be appropriate as an honor gift, than to follow the "rules."

Preparing Tobacco to make Prayer Ties

Tobacco or Prayer Ties

I mentioned earlier that I would describe how to make tobacco ties. First, let me tell you what they are and why we use them. Essentially, these are a physical representation of our spiritual intentions, held out to the forces of the universe, to continually remind them of our request or prayers. They are similar to the prayer candles I have seen in Greek Orthodox churches. The idea there is to say a prayer as you light a special candle that has been "sanctified" or dedicated to holding that prayer up continually for as long as the candle burns.

I work in the bio-medical electronics industry. I understand that one puts the electrical impulse (thought generated by your brain) of your request or prayer into the tobacco or mix that you wrap up inside the "tie." The tobacco then holds the energy of your thought, much like a battery, and continually releases it into the universe until it disintegrates or, in many cases, after a prescribed amount of time, is burned in a special fire.

In the old days, the material used to make a tobacco tie was a small patch of dyed leather and leather, lace, or hair braided into a string. Nowadays, we use colored cloth and string made of cotton or wool. The main thing I have found is they work better if the materials used are natural and clean. The color used depends on what message you are sending up, say red for a request, white as a thanks offering, etc. It all depends on what you are directed to do by the Spirits, as well as what tradition you follow.

There are many ways to make a prayer tie. Some ties are as large as a softball; some are so small it is difficult to even tie them. The way I was taught to make them is in small sizes. I was told that to make them large tends to throw the balance of nature off in the area you leave them. But again, this is just the way I was told.

Before you start, you should smudge yourself and all the things you will be using. The same smudging procedure is used as when loading a Pipe, which is described again in more detail in a later chapter, "Filling and Passing the Pipe."

The first thing I do is burn some flat cedar, to make the area clear of any negativity. Cedar not only repels "bugs" in the physical world, but also in the spiritual. I then smudge everything to be used in the ceremony with sage. Sage is the spiritual counterpart to water in the physical world. It is used to wash away spiritual "dirt". I "wash" myself with the smoke of the sage first. This is done the same way one would prepare to cook food. First, wash your hands, then the "utensils" you will use, including the tobacco bag, which I open and wave some of the smoke into. During the process of creating the tie, sweet grass is kept burning during the actual saying or thinking of the prayer. The smoke of sweet grass draws the attention of the Spirits to your prayers. It provides a sort of pathway for them to follow. I think of it as flower pedals being strewn before royalty, as they enter a room.

Tobacco is used as an honoring to the Spirits who come to help. The tobacco is not burned; it is put into the tie for the Spirits to have.

I hold a square of cloth, maybe two inches by two inches, in the palm of my left hand. Next, I take a pinch of tobacco in between my right fingers and thumb, hold it up to the Great Mystery, and say or think my prayer. As described previously, I am actually transmitting the electrical impulses from my thoughts, out of my brain, down my arm, and into the tobacco through my fingers. This is also how we put our prayers into a Pipe. The prayer is then "stored" in the tobacco, which I wrap up into a little "ghost" shape with the cloth. The tobacco in the middle of the cloth forms the "head" of the ghost and the remainder of the cloth forms the "tail." I then take the string and wrap it around the "neck" of the ghost four times (for the four cardinal directions) and tie it with *only one pass through*, kind of half of a knot.

This is so the prayers can come out of the tie, or possibly so it can come apart when its job is done. To tie it with a complete knot is to lock your prayers up in it until it is changed by fire or decomposed in the future. At that point, the prayers are released into the universe for response.

How many ties you make depends on the purpose of your prayers. I make just one tie, often to say thank you for something that has been done for me. These I leave out until they disintegrate, which may take over a year. Often I make a string of ties, seven in the number, to honor the seven sacred directions of the Cherokee. I know of some Lakota ceremonies where you are required to make over 400 ties all in a row on just one string.

Sometimes your ties are taken into a sweat lodge and hung over your head to be part of your prayers in the lodge. Usually these are burned in the lodge fire right after the ceremony. In some cases they are burned a specific number of days after the lodge has been done, usually three or four days. It is important that someone comes back to the lodge to do this. If this is neglected it can short-circuit your requests.

More often, we use the ties to send up our requests by hanging them in a tree. I always approach the tree I want to hold them for me and ask if it is willing to help in this way. If I get an inner confirmation or good feeling that this tree agrees, I then hang the tie on one of the branches in the appropriate direction to correspond with the intent of the tie itself. An example might be to hang it on the east side of the tree if I am asking for vision or information on something I want to do. Maybe I would hang it on the west side if I were asking for help to walk out my present path of life. If I hang it on the north it might be because I am asking for physical provision or wisdom from the ancestors. There are many different traditions about the directions. You will need to find out what is appropriate for you.

In summation, I encourage you to try making some prayer ties. I have found them to be a very good way to make known our needs to the Great Mystery. The responses to them are often more dramatic than just saying our prayers. Why? I do not know for sure, but my theory is that in making the ties we are incorporating all of creation in asking for assistance. It seems as if this is the current message being emphasized by Spirit of late - the message of *interdependence*. To just pray by yourself is to stand on your own; to ask through a prayer tie is to incorporate the plant people, the tree people, the animals if using wool or leather, etc. It is an acknowledgement that we are all interconnected, that none of us stands alone or apart/above the rest. I think when we acknowledge this need to be interconnected; the Great Mystery is swifter to respond so as to encourage this kind of thought and action.

Awakening the Pipe

Once you have obtained a Pipe, you will want to have it properly awakened. Traditionally, a Native American Elder, a Ceremonial Pipe holder, or other spiritual person does this, which is the most desirable way. But in the case of your personal Pipe, you can do it yourself *if* you do not have any other option. Remember, interdependence.

Elders Adam Fortunate Eagle and Raven Houston preparing for the Awakening Ceremony.

It should be noted the number of directions honored and in what order varies according to which Nation is doing the ceremony. The ways described are just my tradition. Remember, you need to seek instruction from the Pipe also. If it were a matter of just going through the motions of an incantation, you might as well join some dogmatic religion.

This also applies to every time you pray with the Pipe after it is awake. I have been taught to always vary the ceremony a little each time I fill the Pipe, to avoid creating a dogmatic rut, which can hinder the Pipe's ability to fully assist you. You should always seek the input of the Spirit of the Pipe each time you pray with it. The idea is for you to have a vibrant, living relationship with the Pipe instead of a lifeless, powerless, dogmatic ceremony. This causes me to listen to the promptings of the Pipe, rather than just going through the motions like some responsive reading from a pew-back hymnal.

I will share with you the general way I awaken a Pipe. First, I cleanse and purify myself and the new Pipe, unassembled. I purify in a sweat lodge, as this is how I was taught by Adam, who is *Anishinobie.* However, I am a Cherokee and in that tradition we do not use sweat lodges for spiritual purposes. In the case where you do not have a sweat lodge available, you might try the method we Cherokee use to purify ourselves. This method is just you, not the Pipe.

It is called *Going to Water.* Basically you immerse yourself under water in a flowing stream seven times in honor of the seven directions. The colder the water, the better. Because this is not just a physical cleansing but spiritual also, it is highly advised that you have someone assist you when you do this. The effects this will have on you can be quite powerful, and many have been known to be overcome to the point where they have trouble getting out of the water. Your assistant can help you dip under and then assist you in walking back to the shore. If this is the way you chose to purify yourself before awakening the Pipe, it should be followed by a good smudging of both you and the Pipe with sage. Remember, intention is the key. Do this ceremony with conscious thought of the Spiritual beings of the seven directions; do not just go dunk yourself in some water.

Now, back to how I awaken the Pipe using a sweat ceremony. Usually after the sweat, but sometimes during, I will assemble and fill the Pipe for the first time, calling on the assistance of the Spirits of the four sacred directions, and holding the mix towards them. I face each direction and call on East, South, West and North in turn, followed by touching the earth (Mother Earth), lifting a pinch above (Father Sun/Great Mystery) and then finally touching my chest, the place of my own heart/spirit, representing the center or the place where I am. All total I use seven pinches for the seven directions.

At some point during the prayers I invite a Spirit to come take up residence in the Pipe. Often it will give its name and give a sense of the medicine/purpose of the Pipe. Smoking all of the mix and blowing smoke to all the seven directions finishes the ceremony. If done correctly - from a good heart and with respect to the traditions - the Pipe becomes the living body of the Spirit who has come to assist you in your walk.

Filling and Passing the Pipe

There are many different traditional ways of lighting, smoking and handling a Pipe. I will only share the ways that I use. Once again, there is no one correct way and each Pipe will eventually teach you how it wants to be used. Pay attention to what you do and use when the Pipe burns well and also when it doesn't. This is one way it tells you how to care for it.

For instance, I care for a Pipe who wants to be lit only with lightning struck wood. I know of Pipes who do not respond well to butane lighters, or only burn well when lit with a coal from a fire. I also know of many Pipes who can be lit with anything from a lighter to book matches. It all depends on the individual Pipe. Some common guidelines for handling a Pipe follow.

I would like to take you through a step-by-step loading or filling of the Pipe. As I said previously, it is never done exactly the same way twice, but this will give you an idea of how it can be done. I might add here that in some traditions, a special song is sung during the filling of the Pipe. In others, as is in mine, there is no song, but prayers and requests are made in a certain order. Please remember this is the tradition I follow. You will need to work with the Pipe who comes into your care, to find out which method you should follow.

Preparing to Smudge

The following smudging "protocol" is the same one I use when preparing the tobacco ties mentioned previously. The first thing I do is burn some flat cedar, to make the area clear of any negativity. I then smudge myself and everything to be used in the ceremony with sage to wash away spiritual "dirt." After I wash myself, I then pass all items to be used through the smoke to cleanse them. This includes the tobacco bag, which I open and wave some of the smoke into. Lastly, I wash the Pipe itself.

In my tradition, one never blows on any kind of burning smudge, but instead fans it with your hand, feathers or simply by waving it back and forth, to keep it burning. It is considered disrespectful to the Spirit of the herb to blow your breath onto the smudge. After each item to be used in the ceremony is cleansed, I pass the stem of the Pipe through the smoke from East to West, then from South to North, followed by drawing the sage smoke up through the hole in the stem with my mouth. I pass the bowl through the smoke in a clockwise circle, allowing the smoke to enter both holes in it.

Often I will wet the tang of the Pipe (the part that fits into the bowl) with my mouth in order to swell the wood and provide for a good fit and seal. I lift the Pipe bowl in my left hand, the one closest to my heart, and the stem in my right up to the Great Mystery and speak about the symbolism of the male and female being joined to become of great service to all our relations. Part of this thought is not necessarily the joining of a man and a woman, but more in finding the balance of both male and female within oneself. I give thanks for the gift of the Pipe and for all those who were involved in bringing me to it.

I join the two parts and say *"Whe en day Yaa,"* Cherokee for "I am part of the Great Mystery," or the Lakota would say *"Mitakuye Oyasin"* meaning "we are all related." Depending on the Pipe, I then either place it on a rack made of willow with the stem pointing in one of the cardinal directions or I hold the bowl in my left hand and rest the stem in the crook of my left arm. At this point sweetgrass is lit so it burns along with the sage. It is good to try to keep the sweetgrass burning for the entire time I am filling the Pipe. Sweetgrass smoke provides a pleasant pathway for the beneficial Spirits I will be calling on to come and assist me. Sweetgrass is sometimes hard to keep burning and I often ask the assistance of someone to hold it and wave or fan it for me.

Now I start to fill the Pipe with the mixture I have prepared. In some traditions, the mix is prepared fresh before each use on a special platter made just for the occasion. I take a small pinch of the mix in my right hand and move it in a clockwise circle through the smoke of the sweetgrass. I hold it up to the East and ask the Spirits responsible for the things of that direction to come join me in the ceremony. After I ask for their help, I place the mix in the Pipe bowl. A new pinch is used for each direction or prayer.

It should be noted here, aside from the main Spirits who represent each direction, there are Spirits I personally associate with that direction. For instance, I call on the Spirit of the Sun in the East, as does most any tradition. But I also call on a Spirit who has personally helped me in the past but that might not apply to someone else (such as a Spirit like Badger). So, it is I call out towards the East, "Grandfather Sun, would you come and join us in this ceremony today? We need your help." I also call out to the Spirit of Badger, "will you come to our assistance here today? There is a place for you all here in this Pipe, this place of council." In some cases the personal Spirit may be a departed loved one. And so it is I call to the South next and those who live there, then to those in the West, then to the ones in the North.

At this point I kneel down and touch the earth with the mix in my hand, calling on all my relations who dwell in, on, and above my Mother. This is followed by lifting a pinch up to the Great Mystery in the heavens and requesting all who dwell with it come and join us, for there is a place in the Pipe for them also.

Turtle Pipe with cedar and antler stem

Finally, I hold some of the mix to my heart and call on my own Spirit - some call it the higher self - to join in this council, for there is a place in the Pipe for me. I represent all two-leggeds. It is very humbling to realize we have a place in this council chamber next to the greatest beings of Creation, but it is true.

Next I hold a pinch in my fingers and put the requests or prayers into the mix. As I said before, our thoughts are electrical impulses that can be measured. The electrical energy of the thought literally travels from our mind where it is generated, through our fingers, and into the mixture (battery). When it is transformed from physical (the herbs) into spiritual (smoke) by the fire, the thoughts are carried up and dispersed into the whole universe and come to the attention of the Great Mystery.

Now that the Pipe is fully loaded with the mix as well as our requests, I generally light it. Usually a Pipe is lit immediately after it has been filled. This is not always the case, however, as sometimes a loaded Pipe is left on an altar for anywhere from a few minutes or hours to several days, depending on the ceremony. An example of this would be during a sweat lodge ceremony where the Pipe is filled at the beginning of the ceremony but left on an altar until after the sweat is done. Another example is some *Sundance* ceremonies where the Pipes are left on the altar for several days. Most of the time when using a personal Pipe, one smokes it immediately. However, if the occasion arises where it is necessary to let it sit for a while, the following procedure should be followed, as it is done with the Ceremonial Pipes in the ceremonies mentioned here.

In order to keep the prayers and requests that have been put into the bowl uncontaminated by thoughts and events that may occur near it during such times, a "plug" of sage leaves is formed by rolling just the leaves into a ball in between the palms of your hands and put into the bowl on top of the mixture. This is a physical reminder to the spiritual world that the prayers are protected by the Spirit of the sage. The plug is then removed just prior to lighting the Pipe. After the Pipe ceremony has concluded, it is customary to "clean" the Pipe bowl inside and out with the smoke from this plug of sage. After cleansing the bowl, both the hole where the mix is burned, as well as the hole the stem fits into are plugged, in a similar fashion, with new sage plugs. This keeps the bowl uncontaminated until it is next used.

When the time does come to smoke it, I face the East and light the Pipe. I draw the smoke into my mouth but not into my lungs, blowing the smoke down onto the Pipe first, then washing smoke over my head/mind with my hand. I offer smoke to the four directions, starting with the East, by blowing it along the Pipe with the stem pointing towards that direction. After each of the four directions has been addressed, I follow the same pattern as when filling the Pipe. I blow smoke towards Mother Earth, then towards the sky and finally I hold the Pipe bowl to my heart, the last of the seven directions, blowing smoke over the union of my heart and the Pipe.

If there are others present I pass the Pipe around the circle in a clockwise direction, honoring the direction of all life, the direction of the sun. In some traditions, the direction would be counter-clockwise to honor the direction of the migration of a Tribe from Central America, such as the Cherokee or Shawnee.

There may be instances when you may not have enough mix in your Pipe for all to be able to smoke it, either due to the size of the bowl or the number of folks you are sharing it with. In some cases, it is proper to refill the Pipe if the mix runs out. This is done by simply smudging each pinch, as in the original loading of the Pipe, but with one difference. Instead of calling on the Spirits as before (because the Spirits are already here) one simply holds the mix up to the different directions in turn as an acknowledgment, and then puts it into the bowl. If the ceremony or occasion does not call for reloading the Pipe, it is still passed completely around the circle of folks gathered, but the stem is held to each shoulder or the bowl is held to one's heart. In this way all receive the blessing of the ceremony and the Pipe.

If the Pipe makes it all the way around the circle of participants and there is still mixture to be burned, the remainder is smoked until it is all consumed. Both the refilling and/or the final smoking should be done by the one who loaded the Pipe in the first place, thus training him or her to judge how much mix to put in according to the occasion. (Smoking a full bowl by one's self can be somewhat overwhelming, depending on what the mixture is made up of.) I generally smoke every bit of the mix in the bowl, relighting it as necessary. We want all of the prayers to go up to the Creator.

Now that we have almost completed the ceremony, I place the tip of the Pipe bowl to the Earth with the stem pointing towards the East at a 45° angle towards the sky. As I part the stem from the bowl of the Pipe, I speak to the Spirits who have gathered, telling them how grateful we are they joined us. I then send them back "home" with our blessings.

This is a *very important* thing to do. It is always important to be polite to the Spirits. As mentioned previously, putting a Pipe together starts the ceremony and "activates" the Spirits. If you put a Pipe together, you start a chain of events that cannot be stopped, whether or not you actually complete the ceremony. The ceremony has been designed to give a constructive channel or direction for the power set in motion by assembling a Pipe. If that power is not properly directed, it can cause things to go awry. If you do not place an end to the ceremony, the Spirits who have attended may not work in conjunction with your intentions, as they are left "hanging." They may cause mischief or other things in order to get our attention, possibly to teach us to respect them and the traditions we have inherited.

Upon completion of the ceremony, the ashes from the Pipe are mixed with those of the herbs used in smudging and then given back to Mother Earth. If any mix has been spilled during the ceremony, it is gathered and also given back to the Earth. In the event none was spilled, I take a pinch from the pouch and offer it. This is to ensure we will always have the herbs for our Pipes. As a special blessing, sometimes the ashes are rubbed on the forehead or hands of one or more of the participants of the ceremony. As always, each situation will have differences according to the particular reason for the ceremony and the tradition being followed.

As mentioned before, I always end by smudging everything again with sage, letting the smoke enter the holes of the bowl. I then plug them with wads of sage. This will keep the "Council lodge" (the bowl) clean and ready for the next "gathering." Everything is then wrapped, placed carefully back into the Pipe bag, and kept in a safe place until the next ceremony.

Now I will mention a few things which helped me when I was first introduced to the Pipe that may be of assistance to you also. For the first month (new moon to new moon) I had the Pipe, I took time to pray with it every day. Each session was so I could learn what the Pipe's preferences were, sort of to get acquainted with each other. I also slept with the bowl under my pillow for the first month, and have kept it within arm's reach of my bed ever since. I did this so it could speak to me during my dreamtime.

I will add a word of caution at this point. When you sleep with the Pipe bowl under your pillow it will speak strongly to you. The problem is if you sleep with a partner, they will also be affected. When my partner at the time slept with a Pipe she was temporarily caring for, it "talked" all night to the Black Thunder Bird Pipe that I had next to my side of the bed. All night long we both had strong dreams. I felt as if I were caught in the middle of an intense discussion, so to speak. We both kept waking up to loudly audible words like "Thunder," "Bear," and "Healer," etc.

I have found the Pipe will not smoke well for someone who has used drugs or alcohol within 24 hours of a ceremony. It has an uncanny way of humbling those whose egos are not in balance. Always use natural fire, or at least wooden matches, (versus, say, a lighter) to light a Pipe when in the presence of traditional Elders. I often put the glowing coal from some of the sage smudge into the Pipe to light it.

When accepting a Pipe being passed to you, use your left hand to hold the bowl; it is the one closest to your heart. Pass the Pipe in a clockwise direction unless for specific ceremonial reasons you are directed to do otherwise. Usually the one who lights the Pipe will blow or offer smoke to the different directions. Others to whom the Pipe is passed may do various things with the smoke, but in some traditions, it is considered an insult to the caretaker of the Pipe to offer smoke to the directions after they have already done it. It is as if you are saying they didn't do it well enough. I usually have people take four puffs and they can offer it up however they want.

When passing the Pipe to the next person, hand it to them with your left hand on the bowl, bowl first, and your right hand on the stem. When receiving the Pipe, rotate the stem around to your mouth so the stem goes in a clockwise direction, thus completing the circle started by the one who hands it to you. Also, always hold the Pipe by the bowl, not just the stem. This will prevent the bowl from falling off the stem as is passed.

When you draw the smoke into your mouth, do not inhale it. To do so is to take all the prayers back inside yourself, instead of sending them up to the Great Mystery. A stick or tamper often is passed with the Pipe to help keep it burning. This is used to gently tamp the mix down as it burns away, keeping the coal on fresh mix.

Cleaning the Pipe

After the Pipe has been taken apart, and before it is put away, a cleaning rod is run through the stem while the resins are still warm. The bowl is also cleaned out, so the pathway of the smoke will not get clogged. If it does clog up, one way to clean it is to put the bowl in a pan of cold water and *very slowly* warm it up. The resins will turn the water into a "tea" and the bowl may be rinsed out with *hot* water. Some cautions about using this method must be noted. First, both the heating up and the cooling down of the bowl must be done slowly. Think of it as if you are bathing an infant. Also, if the bowl has any metal inlay it could become damaged.

Cleaning the stem with the cleaning rod is usually sufficient. One time I had a friend who had a double-channel Pipe stem, sometimes referred to as a "puzzle" stem. The smoke channel zig-zags so you cannot run a rod through it. Ceremonial Pipes that have a very long stem are made this way so it takes two people to light it, creating *inter*dependence among the participants of the ceremony. This also helps keep the caretaker's ego in check, as it emphasizes his or her need for assistance. My friend and I found two ways to clean this type of stem. The first was to inject hot water through it with a syringe. Remember, though, most stems are two pieces of wood glued together and the hot water may effect it. The second way was to run a guitar string through it. As always, remember you are caring for the body of your Spiritual helper, so do unto it as you would the body of your own infant.

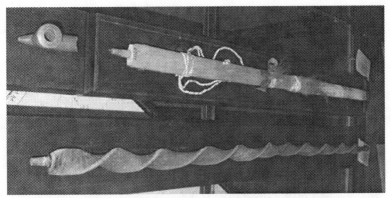

Original stems from the Lewis and Clark expedition

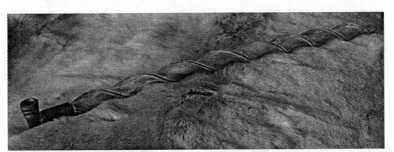

Replica Pipe created for the 200 year reenactment of the welcoming of Lewis and Clark by the Bitterroot Salish. Stem carved by Reggie Boyd, of Retail Flutes, the bowl was carved by the author

Chapter 7
The Personal Pipe

Is the Pipe for You?

So now you have read this book, and are wondering how to know if the way of the Pipe is the right path for you. How can you know? As in any relationship, you have to spend time with someone to get to know what role they may play in your life. Often we are strongly attracted to someone, only to find out later it would be too much for us to be their mate, but being their friend is just right. It is sad when we jump into a relationship too fast and find out later it really isn't the one for us. So it is with the Pipe. I recommend you find someone who has one and spend time with them praying with it. See how you feel about the results, as well as the demands it may put on you personally. Can you make the necessary adjustments you know in your heart will be needed for you to walk together? If the answer is yes and you do obtain a Pipe, even then I recommend you spend a kind of "engagement" period with it. Once you make a commitment to care for a Pipe, it is for life.

I once I had a woman approach me after she had seen a vision of a Pipe during a *Sundance* she was attending. She described a Pipe I had carved, but not yet awakened. It would have been a simple thing for me to just hand her the Pipe based on her vision, but I feel a responsibility towards both the Pipes I create and those who would care for them. I act sort of like a matchmaker. I told her to start attending as many Pipe ceremonies as she could. It was amazing how ceremonies suddenly became available. It took months before I felt she was ready to care for a personal Pipe. She spent those months being around Pipes, attending ceremonies where they were used, and learning as much as she could about them. I believe she felt the attraction, saw a vision, and then proved her commitment to the Pipe. As a result, she was given the responsibility of a very beautiful and powerful Pipe.

In the *Sundance* tradition, you know you are to dance after you have received a vision or dream of yourself dancing. It is confirmed by a vision quest, where you are shown by the Spirits what your dance outfit should look like, etc. Then you prepare for the rest of the year, keeping yourself clean on all levels and working on your dance items. In the same way, you may receive a vision or dream of a Pipe, but this is confirmed by several other things afterwards. I know there always are exceptions and if you are given a Pipe, then you need to find out, as I did with the UN Turtle Pipe, if it has come to you to have you be its caretaker, or maybe just to pass it on to someone else. Remember, it is about having a relationship with a living representative of the Great Mystery, not about ownership.

How Do You Get a Pipe?

So how do you obtain a Pipe? You could receive one as a gift or you can make your own. There are some very good instructions and materials available from the "Keepers." (see the contact information at the end of the book) If you carve your own, it is often the custom to make two Pipes, giving the first one away as a gift before using the one you make for yourself. You could also purchase a Pipe. It is important to understand there are many different feelings about paying money for a Pipe. Since there are hundreds of different Native Nations and each has its own customs concerning the Pipe, I can only present the way my personal Elders and I feel. We feel that as long as a Pipe has never been smoked (awakened) it is acceptable to purchase it. In the pre-contact days, there were those in every village who excelled in various skills: arrow makers, quill workers, vessel makers, as well as Pipe carvers. To carve a Pipe in those days using stone tools took much longer than it does today. A large amount of meat or even a horse might be exchanged for a

Pipe.

Once a Pipe has been awakened (smoked in ceremony), it is the home/body of a Spiritual being, and is considered alive and sacred. Such a Pipe should *never* be sold. I will mention here there is a situation where it *may be* proper to purchase an awakened pipe, but this is a gray area. There are no 100% rules for anything in life or spirit, so with that in mind I offer this "exception" to the rule.

There is one circumstance I am aware of, and possibly others I am not aware of, where purchasing an Old Pipe may be acceptable. If someone who holds the Pipe as sacred comes across an awakened Pipe displayed for sale somewhere, I would think it a good thing for him or her to buy it to release it from its "captivity." I know of a few such cases, and in every one the Pipe seemed to need a lot of cleansing and rededication. They seemed to be "angry" for lack of a better term. I know of one very powerful Pipe rescued in this way and it still took over a year of cleansing it in sweat lodges, with sage, etc., before it could be used in ceremony.

The main thing about purchasing a Pipe under these circumstances is the money is to be considered a sacrifice, and no thought of "ownership" is attached to the purchase. It may very well be that you are paying the price in order to give the Pipe away when you meet the one *it* chooses to care for it. Remember, these old Pipes are sold by collectors for thousands of dollars. Are you ready to pay that kind of money with no thought of ownership? If so, then you are thinking with a Native mind.

What happens to a Pipe when its caretaker dies or fails to pass it on to another? Usually an "active" Pipe may be passed on as a gift or inheritance. Sometimes it is buried with its caretaker after they pass over. Again it must *never* be sold. If you have a Pipe you purchased and it has already been smoked, you should contact an Elder or caretaker of a Pipe to discuss what should be done. No two cases are ever the same, so individual attention is required. Often the "rule" would be to bury the Pipe, but I would caution you to ask the Pipe first and then look for the confirmation of an Elder. As I pointed out in the very beginning of this book, Pipes are coming out of many places to be put back into service around the world.

Pipe Accessories

There are several things that are helpful, and in some cases necessary, to keep with your Pipe. They are sacred just as the Pipe is and not just implements. Often they are made by others and given to the caretaker as gifts *for the Pipe*. These things could include a bag or pouch for the mixture, a rod to run through the stem after smoking to clean it, and a tamper, usually made out of cedar or bone to help tamp down the burning coals in the bowl to keep it going. The tamper I have for the UN Turtle Pipe is shaped like a long thick chopstick with a bird head carved on the end. It is decorated with porcupine-quill work, and was a gift to the Pipe for doing a blessing at a wedding. You will also need various bags to hold matches or flint and steel, as well as the Pipe bag to hold it all in.

The Pipe bag is a very important part of all this. It represents the body that houses the Pipe, and the Pipe itself represents the heart of the body. A Pipe bag can be very elaborate with intricate beadwork or quill work on it. The designs usually represent the medicine of the Pipe, such as the medicine of a Butterfly or the Thunder Beings. Often the bag is made for the Pipe holder by his or her mate. This is to acknowledge the joint responsibility and sacrifice a couple have for the Pipe. In some cases, this type of gift represents the desire of the giver to join the Pipe's caretaker in a life of service to the people, possibly reminiscent of the Lakota *"Chanupa"* (bowl) and *"Calumet"* (stem).

I will mention here that many couples each have their own individual Pipe. When one travels without the other to a ceremony, they will often bring their mate's Pipe with them. The Pipe is put on the altar along with the Pipe of the person who is present, either wrapped in its bundle, or sometimes assembled, so the Spirit essence of the absent mate is present, providing balance and support to the one who is there. Remember the medicine of the Pipe is the bringing into balance the male and female.

Just as a couple who have devoted their lives and relationship to the service of the people multiplies their effectiveness many more times than just by two, the same applies to the two Pipes on the altar together. In some tribes, it was the custom to make a Pipe for the man your wife left you for. This was then gifted to him, to make the statement you never "owned" her and now he was responsible for her well-being, just as he was responsible for the new Pipe. Just as with a Pipe, she is acknowledged as a free agent who chooses whom she will be with. The similes go on and on.

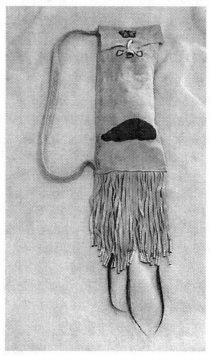

Chapter 8
The Ineffective Pipe

What happens when a Pipe that has been of "uncommon assistance" to you seems to lose its power? Can something cause a Pipe to become less effective?

Even the most powerful of Pipes can have its medicine hindered or even completely destroyed. What can hinder or weaken a Pipe? Anything that hampers the relationship between you and the Pipe. As I said in the beginning of this book, the Way of the Pipe is a lifestyle, not just something done once in awhile.

Those who have experienced this often wonder if something is wrong with the Pipe. On the contrary, the fault usually lies with the humans involved. While it is important to know what to do to protect the Pipe in your care, in order to keep it healthy and in top condition, by far the most common hindrance to its effectiveness is your own intent.

For instance, it is known that drinking alcohol within a certain amount of time before a ceremony will hinder the Pipe's ability to assist you. This is true, not because of some Kryptonite-like quality of the alcohol, but because the alcohol interferes with your relationship with the Pipe. As with any relationship, its effectiveness will be hindered to the extent that those involved do not remain in fresh ongoing communication. Imagine trying to have a meaningful conversation with your spouse the morning after you have "tied one on." You could not expect much quality with that conversation. The same applies to your time communicating (ceremony) with the Pipe.

If a couple lets their relationship get into a rut or neglects to show care for each other, if things become so routine the relationship lacks life, the couple will eventually drift apart. Clear communication with the Pipe is vital, for it to assist you. If you let your relationship with the Pipe get into a rut, or if you neglect the needs of the Pipe, you and the Pipe will drift apart. When the occasion arises where you need assistance and answers from the Pipe, communication will be difficult at best. This is one reason I was taught to alter each Pipe ceremony just a bit, to prevent the ceremony from becoming dogmatic. Come to think of it, that is good advice for any relationship.

I don't want to overlook certain situations and practices which can actually cause damage to a Pipe. These include, improper handling and storage, public display, making the Pipe subject to negative intent, and close proximity with the medicine of a woman who is regenerating her power to create life during her moon time. It is important to protect the Pipe from anything that could actually cause it harm, just as in the same way a man would protect his family from obvious threats. But this same man might easily get so caught up in his job; he neglects their need for his attention and allows their relationship to drift off into something barely alive. The same principle applies to the Pipe. One might take great lengths to ensure it never comes into contact with a woman on her moon, but this same person may also neglect the less pressing needs of the Pipe such as its care and "feeding." The saying fits, "Too busy taking care of the urgent to take care of the important."

There are some fairly universal ways to protect a Pipe from the more obvious things that would hurt it. One must understand these traditions have been developed and followed for centuries because they are real ways of dealing with real issues. Wrap the stem with sage to help keep it clean. I also like to add flat cedar to the stem bundle, as it tends to repel negative spiritual influences. The bowl of my Pipe is always plugged with a wad of sundance sage unless I am cleaning it or using it. This is to keep unwanted energies out of the bowl. As I mentioned previously, I also keep a piece of bear root wrapped up with the bowl. This is to help neutralize the power of a woman's moon time. However, it is only a buffer, not complete protection. I have found the bear root will hold off that energy until I can get the Pipe physically away from the source of potential threat, but only for a short time.

Again, I want to emphasis a woman's moon time is a wonderful and powerful event, not in any way negative. I am not sure why the power of a woman at that time has the effect on things such as a Pipe, tobacco, or other sacred things, but over the centuries it has been proven the two powers should not be mixed. I think it may be partly about keeping our attitude towards the power to regenerate life in proper perspective. I wonder how many of our society's ills are due to lack of proper respect towards women. There is no greater power on this earth than to be able to give life, which is the most distilled physical manifestation of the ultimate power, love.

The Pipe should never be brought out just for display. To do so opens it up to the energies of those around it. I often think of when I took my newborn son into the store for the first time. Everyone wanted to look at him, hold him, etc. All I wanted was to wrap him up, and protect him from even the well-intended attention. I would not let someone hold him unless they had washed and I knew they understood how to hold him properly. In the same way I would never show a Pipe to just anyone. They must first be cleansed by the smoke of sacred herbs and have an attitude appropriate to ceremony before they can look upon it.

There is one area in particular I wish to address concerning the Pipe's effectiveness. This is the issue of tobacco. As before, it has everything to do with attitude and is an example of the "Native mind" view compared to the "non-Native mind."

Many people believe tobacco is a bad thing, killing and enslaving millions. The herb itself is not evil or bad.

Tobacco's divinely created properties are for the benefit of all. It protects other nearby plants against bug infestations, and it has tremendous curative properties. Tobacco was not used for purely pleasurable purposes before European contact, but instead was strictly used as medicine, both in the physical and spiritual realm. Today, like so many other things sacred to us, tobacco has been misused, causing destruction instead of its divinely intended purpose of healing and restoration. As with any medicine, to over-indulge is to risk great harm from a truly beneficial agent.

As discussed in the chapter on tobacco, most traditionalists use a mix of herbs for smoking in the Pipe. However, there are probably more people using commercially produced tobacco in the Sacred Pipe than those using mixtures. It is important to have the correct understanding as well as attitude about tobacco if you are going to use it in the Pipe.

In the pre-contact days, tobacco was raised and traded under very strict procedures. In many of the tribal cultures of North America, there were special "Tobacco Societies" who were responsible for planting, growing and harvesting the sacred herb. Not only did they have the responsibility of the physical care of the plants, but the spiritual care as well. The plot where it was grown was carefully selected to ensure the women of the village would not need to go near it in their daily activities, thereby eliminating any contact with the moon (menstrual) energy. Just walking close to the plants during her moon, a woman could overpower the tobacco's medicine with her tremendous power of the menses. Special songs were sung at the planting as well as throughout the growing season. The health of the tobacco field often reflected the health of the community, and the importance of how it was cared for rested only on the most trusted shoulders.

So, in today's world, how do we show respect for tobacco? Do we smoke it for pleasure without thought or acknowledgement to the plant relative it comes from? Do we abuse it by overindulgence? It is not for me to say if one should or should not smoke tobacco products for pleasure. But, do we take time to offer thanks to where it came from? Just as with the food we eat, if we want to gain the blessings, we must approach it with respect for the plant it comes from, offering simple thanks to its spirit, and consuming it in a thankful and respectful way.

If your Pipe seems to be less effective, you may need to examine your attitude towards tobacco. It is so easy to go buy some at a store with no thought given of the plant it came from. However, if you use tobacco in your Pipe mix, perhaps the Pipe would prefer home-grown or organic tobacco. When I gather plants for the mix I use, it is done with prayers and offerings back to the plants I am taking from. I also get most of the tobacco I use in my mix from a friend who grows it. The plants are nurtured in a good way, and I can feel the difference in the Pipe's reaction. Possibly the additional human contact with the growing plant and the more effort put into procuring it relates directly to the tobacco's effectiveness as a medium of prayer.

Now I will give you an example from my own experience of how the lack of proper attention can hinder a Pipe. As you read in the beginning of this book, I have the responsibility for a Black Thunderbird Pipe, one which has proven very powerful in working with the weather. You would think a Pipe of that magnitude would be above any restrictions that I, as its caretaker, might impose through my own neglect. However, as with all things, we are created to live in interdependence with each other. I need the Pipe and it needs me, all by Divine design. As stated before, to care for a Pipe is a responsibility, not a title or office.

I had just returned home from the annual gathering of Pipemakers in Pipestone, Minnesota, to discover lightening had started a forest fire close to my home. We had not had any rain for several weeks and the fire threatened to become a major one. The fact the fire was just over the other side of the mountain from my home also added to my feeling of urgency. I asked the Thunderbird Pipe if I could request rain with it and the "answer" was affirmative. I planned to do the ceremony that evening after I got home from work and before I was to go out for dinner with my son.

As I went to the lodge on my property to pray, I realized I was missing two things needed for this type of ceremony. The first was a body of water. The second was a woman to bring a balance of energy to the ceremony. Having recently ended a relationship with the woman who usually would have assisted me, I did not have someone to fill this role. I could have asked my daughter to stand in with me, but I didn't want to wait for her to drive over to my place. After all, dinner was waiting at the restaurant!

I decided I could forgo both of these things, but I neglected to ask the Pipe if this was acceptable. I justified my decision with the excuse I didn't want the ceremony to get in a rut.

The ceremony seemed to go well and I felt the requests would be answered. But, I made one more mistake when I ended the ceremony. I didn't sit for awhile and listen to the Pipe for information. I was in too much of a hurry (and too hungry) to give the ceremony/relationship the proper time and concentration it needed (a male trait, I might add, thus the need for a female to bring balance). One can imagine me sitting impatiently with a mate discussing an important issue, when all the while all I am thinking about is dinner.

So, 24 hours later I was sitting with a small group of friends, most of whom had attended ceremonies with the Thunderbird Pipe before. The weather forecast was for a week of clear, hot, dry weather. I was telling them about the request for rain and as we sat there outside, across the sky rolled a thick, dark cloud bank. We all were excited and hoped it would pour rain on the fire. But the clouds brought no rain. Instead, the winds picked up and lightening struck, causing even more forest to burn.

The next morning I asked the Pipe why this had happened, where upon it pointed out the missing parts of the ceremony. I determined to do the ceremony over again and felt urged to do it at a lake located between the fire and my home. As things worked out, my close friend Marnie called and asked to talk about some events in her life. I asked if she would join me in the ceremony and that would give us a chance to discuss her situation as we drove to and from the lake. I explained to her why I was doing the ceremony over again, that I was feeling guilty that because of my lack, the fire continued for another twenty-four hours.

We found a good place on the lake shore and I set up the altar for the ceremony. This lake has lots of power boats on it and can be very noisy, belying the beautiful mountain setting of the lake. As I began the prayers, for some reason all the boats went to the far end of the lake. Many even shut their motors off giving us a peaceful time of prayer. At the end of the ceremony I went to the edge of the lake and struck the Pipe into the earth water and pointed the stem towards the sky water. As soon as I had completed the ceremony two things happened. First, all the boats returned and I commented to Marnie how nice it was they had been "coincidentally" quiet during our prayers. Second, the steadily blowing east-bound wind suddenly and violently reversed its direction. Waves rose up on the lake and the wind almost blew us away.

Marnie was the first to realize the fire would now be burning back over its previous path. At the same time the clouds grew heavy and rolled across the valley, headed directly for the fire. Marnie, in the wisdom of a woman, gently reminded me I might want to listen to the Pipe for an explanation of these events. As I sat quietly in the midst of the windy turmoil, I heard the Pipe say, "Now you will have the answer in twenty-four hours."

That night it rained briefly at my house, and again the next morning, but nothing of any real consequence. But, true to the Pipe's word, exactly twenty-four hours after the ceremony it started pouring! It rained all night and well into the next morning. The fire was extinguished to the extent that officials were able to pull many of the firefighters off that blaze and transfer them to other fires around the state.

This example shows how even the most powerful of Pipes can be rendered ineffective if not properly cared for or heeded. Once I realized my lack and took the time to listen, the requested and expected results of the ceremony arrived in one of the most dramatic answers to prayer I have ever witnessed.

So when you find the Pipe has become ineffective, examine your lifestyle, attitudes, and practices to determine what may be obstructing your relationship with the Pipe. Take time to listen to the Pipe for answers to this dilemma. Then take the necessary steps required to restore the bond between yourself and the Pipe entrusted to your care.

Letting go of the Pipe

There may come a time when the Pipe in your care will decide it is time to go on to be with another. This can happen for many reasons, and should not be automatically considered a sign you have done something wrong. Most Pipes stay with us for a lifetime. However, just as some relationships only serve us for a time, some Pipes come into our lives and stay only until they have completed their purpose and then move on.

Certainly, if you neglect or abuse the Pipe, it will choose to move on, or the Spirit in the Pipe will leave and it will be just an empty shell, but most often, it is just the time has come for you to make room for a new Pipe in your life, one who will bring a different medicine you will be needing.

I have found it more common for Ceremonial Pipes to change caretakers than with personal Pipes, but even with a personal Pipe, it is the choice of the Pipe. The important thing is if the time comes to end your relationship with a Pipe, holding on to it will serve no one. Have you ever stayed in a relationship longer than it served you? The same degrading of the quality of the relationship will occur with the Pipe.

The most important aspect when faced with giving up a Pipe is to have the proper attitude. As discussed previously, one never owns a Pipe, just as one never owns their wife or husband. You are together because you both chose to be together. If one of you decides you need to move on, it is your *right* to do so. But the way one exercises that right is of the utmost importance if the parting is to be a healthy one. It should be done in a proper manner, with the appropriate ceremony, so the parting is beneficial to all concerned.

Everything in life is a circle. It is continuous and goes through repeated cycles. If we viewed relationships as part of an ongoing circle, each one having its own cycle or "life," then we would see the parallel of letting go of a Pipe and letting go of a spouse as a beneficial thing. Unfortunately, in our society we see a breakup or divorce as a horribly painful and destructive thing, which most often it is. Again, we need to re-educate our minds to think in a Native way, one that recognizes both autonomy and the necessity of change at the completion of a cycle.

If a couples separation were done in a kind and respectful way, with a kind of leaving with integrity, then our lives, as well as our society, would be very different. I am not saying there is not sorrow at the separation, be it with a spouse or a Pipe, but we would be far more accepting of the necessity of the parting with the proper attitude-one that recognizes holding on would only destroy the beauty of what had transpired between the pair.

It is a lost art today to be able to recognize when something has come full circle and it is time to move on to another experience. How much better would you get along with an ex-spouse if you had recognized the ending of the cycle of your relationship and separated before things went sour?

The Pipe is reminding us of what we already know deep inside. If more people treated each other with the kind of respect we show to the Pipe, there would be far less pain and sorrow in our relationships. In the words of a wise Shawnee Elder, "It is more important to be kind to one another, than to be in love with one another." This doesn't sound very romantic, but it is true.

If the personal Pipe in your care does require you to let go and pass it on, there are several traditions that are followed in doing so. The bowl is made of stone that represents the permanent, ongoing aspect of life. The stem represents the temporal aspects of life. One of these traditions is to make a new stem for the old bowl (This is not generally done with a Ceremonial Pipe). The old stem would stay with the one passing the bowl on and be kept on their personal alter. Many times it would be buried with them if they have crossed over. Thus, when a Pipe is passed on, a new stem is carved to represent its new life, and is adorned by the new holder with representations of their own individual medicine. Often the passing of the Pipe is done in a sweat lodge or during a special Pipe ceremony.

Many times the whole Pipe will be "retired" to a private altar. This is done when it is "worn out" or, more accurately, when the spirit in the Pipe is done with its work and leaves it. When the spirit of a Pipe leaves the physical shell it may also be buried, just as one would with the body of a person whose spirit has left.

But obviously, this would only happen if the leaving of the first man were done in a kind and gentle way. All in all, if you are called on to pass a Pipe to another, think of it in terms of putting a special loved one in someone else's care, for the benefit of the humans as well as for the benefit of the Pipe.

A sign of hope

Concluding Notes

In summing up this book, as I said at its beginning, if something is real, it works, and if it works, it is real.

The Pipe is a divine gift to us and it works, not because we have faith that it will, but because it is a real, living entity that takes action independent of us, or if we are fortunate, interdependent with us. We are privileged to be invited to participate with the Pipe in mending the broken hoop of life! If you find the Pipe does not bring the described blessings into your life, perhaps it is not for you. But if you find it is a powerful agent of the Divine for you, I encourage you to build on the small foundation given to you through this book. Go and find others –Elders - who live a daily life with the Sacred Pipe. Observe them and learn, but always remember the truest teacher you will have is the Pipe who has come to live with you - your personal Pipe.

About the Author

James Medicine Tree is a voting Council member and spiritual advisor for the "Keepers of the Sacred Tradition of Pipe Makers" and serves on the advisory board for the E.T. Seton Institute (Black Wolf). Jim is also a well known stone sculptor and Pipe carver. He is responsible for the care of the United Nations Turtle Pipe, created and presented to the UN in 1978 by Adam Fortunate Eagle.

Jim's training in the care of the Sacred Pipe has been with several Elders representing different Nations besides the Cherokee. This has given him a broad perspective on the ways of the Pipe, and it is from this collection of information that he offers the material presented here. His Elders of influence are Adam Fortunate Eagle, spiritual leader of the "Keepers," the late Lilly Windrider Nevarez, member of the Cherokee Medicine Society; M. Running Deer, an Apache spiritual leader, and the late Larry War Eagle, a Cherokee spiritual leader.

Jim resides in northwestern Montana, where he assists with the Good Nations Pow Wow, as well as many other Native cultural activities of the area.

Adam Fortunate Eagle and the author, Jim Tree

Contact the Author

E-mail: jimtree3@yahoo.com

Web sites:
www.wayofthepipe.com
http://www.jtreepipes.bravehost.com
Jim Tree, PO Box 103, Hamilton, MT. 59840

Pipe Making Instructions and Materials

Website: www.pipekeepers.org
1-888-850-8675

The Way of the Sacred Pipe
Copyright © April 1, 2004
By James Medicine Tree

Printed in the United States
107717LV00002B/16-24/A